Their Rightful Place

an essay on children, families and childcare in Canada

Loren Lind
and
Susan Prentice

Canadian Cataloguing in Publication Data

Lind, Loren Jay, 1937–
  Their rightful place

(Our schools/our selves monograph series ; no. 9)
Includes bibliographical references.
ISBN   0-921908-10-5

1. Child care services – Canada. 2. Child care – Canada.
I. Prentice, Susan, 1961– . II. Our Schools/Our Selves
Education Foundation. III. Title. IV. Series.

HQ778.7.C3L5 1992   362.7'12'0971   C92–093674–1

This book is published by Our Schools/Our Selves Education Foundation, 1698 Gerrard Street East, Toronto, Ontario, M4L 2B2.

For subscribers to *Our Schools/Our Selves: a magazine for Canadian education activists*, this is issue #22, the sixth issue of volume 3.

The subscription series Our Schools/Our Selves (ISSN 0840-7339) is published 8 times a year. Publication Mail Registration Number 8010. Mailed at Centre Ville, Montréal, Québec.

Design and typesetting: Tobin MacIntosh.

Cover photo: Lynn Haines with children at the Friends Daycare Centre, Toronto, 1991.

Our Schools/Our Selves production: Heather Alden, Loren Lind, Doug Little, David Livingstone, Tobin MacIntosh, George Martell, Mary Ann O'Connor, Susan Prentice, Harry Smaller.

Printed in Canada by La maîtresse d'école inc., Montréal, Québec.
Copyright © Our Schools/Our Selves Education Foundation
February 1992.

Acknowledgments

We gratefully acknowledge the welcome we received from childcare advocates and workers at daycare centres and the time they gave explaining the intricacies of the system in which they work. We want to especially thank Lynn Haines at the Friends Daycare Centre in Toronto for all her assistance. The staff of the Resource and Research Unit at the University of Toronto were invaluable to the documentary research. Many of the ideas in this book were worked out with the support and encouragement of our editor, George Martell, and through many conversations with Catherine Kellogg and David Holmes. We also received valuable suggestions from Joey Noble and a very useful final reading of the manuscript from David Livingstone. Although the authors share responsibility for the whole book, in the early drafts Susan Prentice contributed Chapters One and Five, and the first part of Chapter Three, and Loren Lind developed Chapter Two, the second part of Chapter Three, and Chapters Four, Six, and Seven.

Loren Lind
Susan Prentice
Toronto, 1992

Contents

Chapter One   *1*
   A Clash Of Values

Chapter Two   *19*
   Children's Gifts

Chapter Three   *44*
   Family and Home

Chapter Four   *65*
   The Childcare Crisis

Chapter Five   *88*
   A Brief History of Childcare Services

Chapter Six   *98*
   Political Responses

Chapter Seven   *118*
   Organizing for the Future

Chapter One

A Clash Of Values

Childcare lies at the centre of a knot of personal and political contradictions, dilemmas and delights. Attempts to untangle this knot lead us back to some of the most basic questions: What are our responsibilities to each other? Who and how shall we care for those who are in need? What is the proper division between personal and public lives? How shall we understand the relationship of the individual to the society she lives in? And where, in all this philosophizing, do we place our children?

Answers to these questions could provide a foundation for social life. However, because we live in a capitalist economy, the market demands of production and consumption, the power of national and international capital and the overall imperative of profit take precedence. Governments and nations—and therefore schooling, welfare services, legal systems, etc.—have to juggle the conflicting requirements of human needs and the needs of capital. In this balancing act, the needs of capital nearly always get the higher priority.

So childcare is caught between the opposing poles of human need and capital accumulation. On the one hand, caring is intimately tied up in how we define ourselves, in our loving and intimate relationships, in the parts of our lives where, if fortunate, we freely choose and feel cherished. On the other hand, care is also an integral part of how our economy reproduces itself, the demands of labour and the profit-making system. How are we to deal with this clash? There are many ways this dilemma could be solved. Within an unfettered capitalism, we could simply contract out all the labour of care. We already buy and sell many aspects of our lives in the buying and selling of labour and goods. We already commodify "love", "care", and "home." We can buy sex and touch through prostitution; concern and loving listening through a therapist; tidy homes and clean clothes by hiring a housekeeper. We can find love or relationships through singles' clubs; we eat in restaurants; we buy entertainment at the theatre; we keep fit at the health club; we find escape at the pub. Perhaps more troubling, we pack away old people into nursing or retirement homes. We send those with psychiatric problems or physical handicaps to total institutions. We warehouse law-breakers within jails. We police the poor with social workers and the welfare network.

These are bureaucratic and commercial solutions—really corporate solutions—to the "inconveniences" of life. Now, clearly some people have much more access to these troubled pleasures than others. Only the affluent can afford to pay for those aspects of life that most working class and middle class people still do for themselves. Other people—poor, working class, native—must endure more surveillance and policing than others as well as face the heavy hand of state welfare services.

Within this framework we could also establish a daycare system. We could build a giant holding tank at the end of every street, fill it with soft and non-toxic toys, install a good video monitoring system and automatic juice dispenser. We could then hire one underpaid young woman to oversee the hundreds of kids, who would be there as our clients. Children could be dropped-off in the morning, picked up at night, and their bills paid at the end of the week. No worries.

This is, of course, a nightmare. At least for most of us. We feel outraged at the thought of bringing a market economy into those parts of our lives that seem most removed from the cash nexus. While many of us have, somehow, come to accept that it is a common-sense thing that criminals need jails, that the elderly need nursing homes and that the mentally ill need institutions, we balk at institutionalizing our small children. The arguments about daycare rage ferociously: "Daycare centres are bad for children!" "Children need their mothers!" "Kids in daycare become juvenile delinquents!" "Maternal deprivation!" "Immoral, damaging, inhumane!" "The state is invading the family!"

There is, on the other hand, an old-fashioned conservative (non-corporate) position on how to arrange for the care of children that has its own particular destructiveness. In small, single-family homes, we could ensure a stay-at-home mother and a working father, with their two or three children. We could give back to men the unquestioned authority and power that several decades of feminism has worked agonizingly slowly to undo. We could re-instate a family wage: Dad would work and Mum would get an allowance. Isolated, alone, going half-mad with the feminine mystique of lonely motherhood and housework, women could care for children. In this world, women would relinquish their claim to independence and men would assume it. Boys would grow up to be patriarchs, and girls would grow up into women who were their adored helpmates. In this model, the world would consist simply of suburban nuclear family havens in a desert landscape. The nuclear family would be everything.

Not only is this kind of nuclear family sexist and unequal, it also conceals what is really going on. When we say a woman is being "cared for" by a man, what we really mean is that she is economically dependent on him, and that she is responsible for his emotional and physical well-being as well as for that of their children. The one put forward as being the "provider" has become in fact the primary receiver.[1] This arrangement carries very high psychic and personal costs to women. And, while men are not oppressed by this gender arrangement—since they are the overt beneficiaries of it—men's innate capacities for intimacy, nurturance and care are also stunted. In a world where "family is everything", all of us—women, men and

---

1. Graham, H. 1983. "Caring: A Labour of Love." In (Eds.) J. Finch and D. Groves. *A Labour of Love: Women, Work and Caring.* Routledge and Kegan Paul: London. p. 25.

children—are necessarily forced to abandon the greatest part of our sociability: our longing for widely-flung and diverse community links.

So neither the corporate model of childcare, nor the romanticized nuclear family adequately meets our needs. In both, there are fundamental problems. In the corporate version, we are "desocialized": made flat, de-personalized, cookie-cutter figures; with bureaucratic provision treating us identically, churned into equivalents, turned into numbers and statistics. In the romantic patriarchal vision, we are saturated in familialism: drenched in one-dimensional gender roles, cut off from larger social relationships, and steeped in a private, individual isolation.

Is there any real choice besides these two scenarios? That is, is there a choice that isn't simply mitigating the inhumanity of these positions, rounding off their harder edges. Is there a choice that stands for something very different?

What Is Common-Sense?

As we search about for alternatives, we look to common-sense to guide our actions. But public daycare seems to go against the "natural" and "normal" way to arrange life. It contradicts common-sense notions about family, the public/private spheres, the different roles of women and men, and the needs of children. In fact, public provision of childcare services seems to turn common-sense on its head.

What about this common-sense wisdom? Even a passing knowledge of history shows how variable the content of common-sense is. Everyone used to "know" that night air was bad for one's health. It used to be widely accepted that the wanderings of a woman's womb in her body "caused" her irrationality. Doctors were certain that some people were more influenced by their bile, while others were more sanguine. Everyone "knew" that belching smokestacks were safe, because nature could safely accommodate all abuses. During the Industrial Revolution, everyone "knew" that children under ten years of age often made better workers, because their small size meant more of them could be fitted into a factory.

Today, everybody "knows" that mothers are "naturally" the

best persons to take care of children, that heterosexual and nuclear families are the best homes possible, and that men and women are always and forever opposites. We "know" that the capitalist economy is the fairest and most efficient system in the world. We are sure that a world of work that goes from 9 to 5 (for the middle class, at least) is not at all a problem in a world where the school system goes from 9 to 3—because we "know" that somehow, some woman will pick up the slack. We know that a "two-wage earner" family means one in which a married woman works, because we "know" that women's labour force participation is optional and expendable within the family. We "know" that experts and professionals know what they are doing and that the scientific research on child development is accurate, unbiased and applies equally across all races, cultures, and religions, holding equally true for girls and boys.

Or do we?

This book makes an argument for a different kind of common-sense. The common-sense developed here reverses the usual priority given to the market by giving it instead to real human needs. This, of course, is a clue to politics: when the market comes first, people and their real and diverse needs, must come second. This is because everyone "knows" that life is a race and that there can only be one winner.

But, a competitive, individualistic, capitalist system of winning and losing is only one of a thousand possible ways of arranging the world. There are alternatives. However overwhelming the task of re-thinking our lives might seem, it is crucially necessary. The Italian marxist Antonio Gramsci said it called for "pessimism of the intellect, and optimism of the will." In this, he meant that one needed a ferocious and vigorous critique of the existing arrangements and a wildly passionate and hopeful conviction that the enormous powers of human creativity and ingenuity could be put to different ends. This book is an essay in that optimism of the will.

Critique has an undeservedly bad reputation: it is associated with being negative, picky, pessimistic and unsatisfied. But in the finest tradition of thoughtful analysis, critique is the ability to kick away the props of common-sense to find out what lies beneath the everyday world. In this task, dissatisfaction can be a useful ally. There is much to be dissatisfied with about the current distribution of power and subordination. To be satisfied requires a smug complacency. Politics are an issue for all of us—the challenge is to find a way to enter and get involved.

Reflection, interpretation, and analysis are the tools we need to figure out what is going on around us. Once "the personal is political," those same skills of insight and sober judgment ordinarily used in politics also need to be applied to our personal lives. This disrupts both our personal lives and the larger world of public policy, and considerably complicates the question of how to achieve social change.

In fact, once we have peeked beneath common-sense, the world no longer looks divided into closed compartments of public and private that we take for granted. Where you stand influences what you see: each location of class, gender, and race influences how the world is experienced. For example, "the private" is usually taken to be the life of intimate relations and recreation at home, while "the public" is the world of work and politics. But all this looks, and is, very different to a single mother on welfare and a wealthy businessman. His family is private, protected, a "haven." Her family is regulated, supervised, made into casework by welfare workers. His work is separate from his home; her work is her home.

There are practical consequences to the split in family experience, with most men in families reaping the pleasant benefits of leisure and being cared for. In one Australian study, researchers found a full half of fathers won't change a baby's diaper.[2] A 1983 study in "liberated" Sweden found that men did an average of less than an hour a day of household chores and/or childcare, whereas women worked over 40 hours/week.[3] In the US, fathers average less than sixty minutes each week in sole care of their children, and in one typical week, 80% of fathers were never alone with their children.[4] In fact, over 60%

---

2. Lamb, M. (Ed.) *The Father's Role: A Cross-cultural Perspective.* Lawrence Earlsbaum: New Jersey. p. 340.

3. Lamb, p. 122.

4. Gagi, A. and M. Lamb, (Eds.). 1983. *Fatherhood and Family Policy.* Lawrence Earlsbaum: New Jersey. p. 143.

of American fathers surveyed had *never* taken sole care of a child. A Canadian survey discovered that husbands with working wives performed even less household labour than husbands with non-working wives.[5] For a taste of this "leisure gap," it is worth noting that in a 1984 Canadian survey half the men reported doing regular domestic work yet less than a third of the women reported getting regular help.[6]

So, the presumed great divide between the world of work and the world of non-work is only true for men. Men in families get real and material benefits from women's labour—and this, in great part, is organized around children and childcare. This point is central to the dilemma of women's oppression within the family.

We make other common-sense assumptions about the home. One of the myths is that we are safe inside our homes and that danger is only in the outside world. The sad evidence, however, points in exactly the opposite direction. In 1983, it was estimated that 50–60% of Canadian families experienced some form of violence. Further evidence of the abuse endured and perpetrated by family members is offered in Chapter 3.

This research reveals a shocking picture, which forces us to ask: what exactly are we trying to save when we want to protect the family? What are we to make of an ideology and practice of family which wants to safeguard such hurtful and harmful relations? There is no avoiding the reality that families are dangerous places for many women and children. And yet, for many people, family is a real refuge from a harsh world. Eli Zaretsky has said that it is a "tragic paradox" that the bases of love, dependence and altruism in human life and the historical oppression of women and children have been found within the same matrix.[7] How can public policy work to change this terrible truth?

Women's and men's strikingly different experience of home and family is a clue that the divide—that of public and pri-

---

5. Anderson, K. et al. 1987. *Family Matters: Sociology and Contemporary Canadian Families*. Metheuen: Toronto. p. 128.

6. Anderson, p. 133.

7. Zaretsky, E. 1982. "Family and the Origins of the Welfare State." In (Eds.) B. Thorne and M. Yalom. *Rethinking the Family*. Longman: New York. p. 193.

vate—is not so cut and dried as we might assume from common-sense. One historian has pointed out that far from the state "invading" or "replacing" the family, a certain kind of alienated public life and a certain kind of alienated private life have expanded together.[8] The form in which the welfare state expanded was public, but the content was private. When we contrast "the public" to "the private" as though they were worlds apart, we obscure their connectedness.

There are a thousand ways that the state and the family are inter-twined, not separate at all. From family allowances and baby bonuses to the tax system of deductions and spousal benefits; from welfare regulations about parent treatment of children to the legal requirements of schooling; and from public planning regulations which stipulate legal from non-legal dwellings, it is absolutely clear that families are widely regulated by the state. There is no crystal clear division between public and private—just shifting, zig-zagging and changeable boundaries.

The problem of childcare may seem dizzyingly far away from this survey. But one thing does emerge clearly: "common-sense" often obscures, rather than clarifies, the problems and potential solutions to these dilemmas. To provide the very best for our children and ourselves, we must reconsider the families in which children live, the relationships they form with adults and community, the relationships of adults to the world of work, the similarities and differences between women and men, and the role of the state in a capitalist economy. And, in this reconsideration, we must insist that things could be done differently.

A Base To Build On

What can help us in this reckoning? In Canada, we are privileged to have a long tradition of radicalism: farmers' movements, trade unionism, over a century of strong women with feminist convictions, the early Co-operative Commonwealth Federation and the more recent New Democratic Party, long-standing ethnic and cultural solidarity groups. Each of these traditions contributes an alternative voice. They have worked to develop a common-sense that puts human life and commu-

---

8. Zaretsky, 1982: 193.

nity first, ahead of economic individualism. They consider human needs before the needs of commerce. These are the values on which this book draws.

Human needs, however, are a complicated concept. Certain needs only emerge under certain historical conditions; other needs are fundamental to human life. What some people need because of lack is directly related to some other people's overconsumption. It is not enough to say that we "need" this or that service or product. What must happen is that we tackle the origins of the need itself. In doing this we show a simple need to be a complex issue. This is a politics of needs interpretation, not merely needs satisfaction.[9]

For example, the "eight-hour working day" was a demand raised by trade unionists in the early part of the century. An eight-hour day would ensure that male workers were not fatigued and at risk in unsafe working conditions, and it would guarantee that they would have time to spend with their families. At base, it was a workers' demand that the market should not dominate all of human life. Feminists today point out that we "need" pay equity and affirmative action for equally complicated reasons. They are necessary because the market streams women and men into different kinds of work, because some work is considered more valuable than others, because women deserve to be paid a decent wage, because employers should not be allowed to be despotic tyrants, and because social justice criteria must govern the private wage contract.

Why do we need childcare? Childcare is a very "compressed" issue: once the box is opened, a thousand reasons spring out. When we consider childcare as an *issue*, not merely a demand, we uncover a great deal about the organization of the world. We need childcare for diverse reasons. We need childcare to enable women who are mothers to enter the paid labour force. We need childcare to share the social labour of raising the next generation. We need childcare as a way of supporting parents, more equitably distributing the tasks of caring between women and men, and offering primary care-givers precious

---

9. Fraser, N. 1989. "Women, Welfare and the Politics of Needs Interpretation." In *Unruly Practices: Power, Discourse and Contemporary Social Theory*. University of Minnesota Press: Minn.

time-off to revitalize. We need childcare as a way of reinvigorating the broader social world. Childcare can help to give non-parents a meaningful way to have relationships with children. Childcare can extend loving relations, opening up the possibility of different kinds of caring. Children need childcare as a way of meaningfully connecting to other adults and children. Mainly, we need childcare as a way of improving the quality and extending the choices in people's lives. These are the reasons we fight for childcare: we want to shape the world to meet our needs.

These are our reasons for needing childcare. We also have our own reasons for not wanting childcare. We don't need childcare as another way of policing marginal families: of regulating working class or single parents. We don't need childcare as "head-start" programmes, designed to remedy the expert judgments that native or poor or immigrant or inner-city families are defective. We don't need workfare coercion that forces parents into the paid labour market, even if they would rather stay at home. We don't need twenty-four hour childcare simply to allow factories to run all night long. We don't need daycare as part of government policies to persuade women to have babies as a patriotic sacrifice for the economy. These kinds of reasons would be an imposition on our choices.

To walk a steady path through the tangled questions of childcare means to hold all these possibilities and risks in mind at all times. It is to steadfastly refuse to concede to the market the power to control our lives. It is to assert, again and again, that public provision can be positive, enabling and chosen in our lives. It is to insist that ordinary people have the right to support and assistance from others and from our governments. It is to refuse the logic of the market and the forces of profit. It is to claim the very best for our children and our selves as a part of our heritage.

In the struggle for childcare we affirm that women and men, children and adults, need relief from the impositions of oppressive common-sense. In a rich country like Canada, it is appropriate to demand that everyone should benefit from the wealth of the country.

An Issue/A Policy

This book discusses childcare as an issue, not just as a policy demand. The next chapter, "Children's Gifts," proposes a new way of thinking about children and their growth from infants into adults. It reminds us that children come bearing gifts: that adult-child caring relationships give, or could give, to adults as well as to children. Children's status in society is deeply ambiguous: they are both revered and ignored. Neither of these perspectives provides a solid foundation for treating children well in either personal or public life. Instead, we need a hard-nosed realism about the role of love and power and the ways they shape children's development and opportunities in social life.

Chapter Three, "Family and Home," develops a historical argument about the variability of families. It shows that "family" is a word which carries two very different meanings. One meaning refers to the *idea* of family, to the ideology of familialism and to our judgments about what families should be. The second meaning of "family" refers to our actual households. The meaning of households, as well as the world inside them, has changed enormously over the past century, in ways that can be largely explained by the needs of the economy and the state. This chapter reviews over a century of Canadian history to explore the changing family. It shows that both the idea and the practices of families and childcare have been regulated by interests other than those of most working class people and women.

Chapter Four, "The Childcare Crisis," provides information on childcare arrangements in Canada. It reviews the provision of services and how they are funded, paying particular attention to the provincial patchwork. It reviews the different roles that municipal, provincial and federal governments play in licensing and regulating care. The organization of childcare services occurs in such a way that provision of "spaces" is—in practice, if not always in theory—more important than the experience children have in programmes. In the debate over "quality" and "quantity", quality tends to be transformed into a technical problem, instead of forming the heart of the service. What becomes clear is that there are fundamental problems in a fee-for-service, free enterprise model of care. There is a deep contradiction between the system of services currently available for purchase or subsidy on the market and the care we need and wish we had.

Chapter Five offers a very brief overview of the history and politics of childcare services and childcare organizing in Canada. It reviews the various forces which have operated to place childcare on or off the public agenda. It tracks these developments simultaneously, to show how childcare advocates have fought for childcare services. By examining this history, we can see how the childcare movement gained its present shape and momentum. This helps us to better understand the way the state has relegated childcare, like other welfare services, to the political margins of public policy.

Chapter Six examines contemporary government responses to the childcare crisis. It reviews recent federal government proposals—the Katie Cooke Task Force and the Martin Special Parliamentary Committee—to show the limits of the Liberal/Tory spectrum of childcare. Neither liberal nor conservative welfare models are adequate ways of organizing childcare. In user-fee services, daycare is a market commodity like any other. The government's support for profit-making daycare shows its corporate committment predominates over human needs. Daycare advocates, battling on the one hand against daycare entrepreneurs and trying to jump-start governments on the other, have proposed an entirely new way to conceive of childcare. This includes reorganizing the micro-politics of service

Chapter Seven, "Organizing for the Future," is where it all comes together in a new vision for childcare services. It reviews some of the dimensions of the quality care which we will want to implement in a national childcare system. The slogan used by daycare advocates is a long mouthful:

> "Free, universally accessible, publicly-funded, non-compulsory, high quality, non-profit, community-based childcare services for every child who wants or needs it."

It isn't catchy, and it doesn't fit easily on a button, but every phrase is important. Each detail in the demand is key: there is no way to take the pieces apart without violating the vision of the whole. But before we closely examine this demand, we have to remember all of the compressed issues contained in the challenge of childcare.

"Free..."

Caring for children is technically "free" in both senses of the word, right now—if you ignore the sacrifice. No one pays mothers to look after kids. Much of the labour of care is done as a labour of love—done for free. And, every woman is also technically "free" to be a mother. But the habitual equation of women with children is part of the way women are oppressed. It is also how the family is partitioned off from the rest of society.

"Free childcare" means publicly funded services that are free of cost at the point of delivery. They will have to be paid for in some way, of course, because good daycare is expensive. The commodity model of daycare reinforces the private nature of the arrangement. In contrast, free daycare is a public recognition that childcare is a public good. If childcare services were free they would join other entitlements in Canadian society. Like education and health care, childcare should be a part of every citizen's entitlement—without a user fee.

"Free" daycare would break the association of childcare with poverty and the "deserving" poor, re-framing it as a need for all families and children. Children need access to care regardless of a caregiver's employment status or income. Free daycare would break the association of childcare with welfare too. There would no longer be bureaucratic hoops to jump through: subsidy requirements to meet, welfare casework involvement, scrutiny by municipal governments. The same way we need publicly provided health care and education in Canada, we also need free daycare.

In the short-term, during the transition to a system without user fees, funding will be required. This is where the demand for a direct grant comes in—so that the parents who now pay the full cost of childcare will have to pay much less. Advocates have called for direct grants as the first step in the direction of full public funding.

"...Universally Accessible..."

Free services are all very well, but they mean nothing if they are not accessible. Universal accessibility has several dimensions. First, it means that the services must exist and that they must be available to all. This means that the scale of provision needs to massively increase. There must be a childcare space available when and where needed. All children's needs must be met: infants, toddlers, pre-schoolers and school-age children, as well as children with special needs. This requires a whole range of service models, too: full-day licensed programmes, private family-home daycare, after-school programmes, drop-in centres, and more. And services must be available in a variety of locations to enable choice to be meaningful. Parents must be able to choose between neighbourhood or workplace care or other combinations of appropriate provisions.

There is a second dimension to universal accessibility: it must be flexible and responsive to the diverse needs for services which families bring. Obviously this will include part-day or part-week care, and after-and-before school care. It might also involve weekend care and overnight care for children in families with shift work or parents who travel. For example, on school professional development days or during summer holidays special services may be required.

This has particular meanings in different regions. Outside of urban areas, rural childcare services may require a transportation system or special remuneration for at-home care. Childcare services in agricultural areas may require seasonal adjustment. In areas of low population density, standards or regulations may need to be altered. In culturally diverse communities, this may involve culturally appropriate services, in the first language of children. For children with special needs or disabilities, special provisions may also be necessary.

"...Publicly-funded..."

A free daycare system is one without user fees. A daycare system without user fees will require massive infusions of public funds. The direct funding of a childcare system stands in direct opposition to the preferred Tory option of assisting families through tax schemes.

Part of public funding will involve the redirection of funds away from programmes like the Child Expense Deduction and into direct programmes. To be fair, this will also require an overhaul of the whole structure of taxation. This will necessarily relate to the division of power and government involvement in childcare and may have implications for standards. In a wealthy federal state like Canada, it seems appropriate to retain high levels of federal funding, which augment the cash resources of poorer provinces. Certainly the municipal property tax base is inadequate to the task of supporting a childcare system. Like the Canada Health Act, which has ensured equity in health care across the country, we must ensure that the care of children in, for example, the less-affluent Atlantic provinces is as good as it is in central Canada. And certainly the legitimate demands on the federal government by native people for self-government must take the costs of their childcare services into account.

We want to create an effective, publicly-funded childcare system, characterized by equity and excellence.

"...Non-compulsory..."

Childcare services must not be compulsory. In this phrase, we recognize the coercive power of services and the danger that parents—mothers, in particular—may be forced into the labour market if they cannot "justify" staying at home. To this degree, we want to protect the privacy of the family and the choices of its members. Just because free, high quality childcare services will exist in ready access in all neighbourhoods is no prescription that all children must use them. Some parents of infants, for example, may choose to take advantage of extended parental employment leaves. And those who feel it is better to care for their children at home should be free to do so—with support. Families with school-age children might want to negotiate flexible hours to match their children's school day. We must ensure that diversity and freedom of choice do not disappear, but are strengthened in a universally accessible system.

".... High Quality..."

Quality is the elusive but absolutely central key to the whole childcare puzzle. On one critical level this relates to standards and regulations, to staff-child ratios, to physical plant requirements, to sanitation, to programming, to staff training and development, and a raft of technical particulars.

Yet, high quality also captures something more. It requires that childcare workers be well paid with good benefits and that the work they do is accorded the respect it deserves. In part, this will mean that men take a career in Early Childhood Education seriously: currently less than 4% of Canadian daycare workers are men. It means, too, that parents must feel confident and comfortable with their children's programme and teachers. It means adequate toys and good quality nourishing and tasty food. It means that programming is culturally sensitive and promotes egalitarian values: that girls and boys of all races and classes are treated as being equal in their potential, their value, and in their contributions to each other and the community.

But more than this, a concern for high-quality care will be a constant source of innovation and new development. We will want to better our programmes, to improve our ratios, to consider standards as minimums rather than as ceilings. In a system where the need for cost-cutting and scraping by has been eliminated via public funding, we can re-direct resources into the quest for the very highest quality of care and best conditions for all participants.

"....Non-profit..."

The profit motive is a killer of quality in a daycare centre. Commercial daycare is a way of keeping childcare services inside the logic of the market economy. The vision we are promoting here is of a different way of caring for each other. In the move towards the gift economy, away from the cash nexus, we do not want to retain the commodity form.

Some programmes, while technically run under the legal auspices of a non-profit programme, may be just as alienating and removed from democratic parent, staff and child input as the worst MacBaby Skool franchise. This is why we need programmes which are community-based while also guided by federal and provincial standards.

"...Community-based...."

Margaret O'Brien Steinfels has pointed out that questions of parent and community control may seem like marginal details about administration. "But," she argues, "the question of parental and community involvement is in fact the single most important, albeit acrimonious, discussion about childcare. It asks, in effect, 'Who will raise our children?'" It is central to the key issue of quality.

Democratic practice is back on the agenda of the social change movement like never before. Over two centuries of experience with the limits of representative democracy have shown that simple elections and representation don't do enough to involve people in decision-making. In a similar way, the notion of "parent involvement" in the administration of a daycare centre is a pale substitute for meaningful control and participation.

Now clearly, the luxury of attending meetings and getting directly involved in a programme requires time and resources which are distinctly unevenly distributed across class, race and gender divisions. But even with a recognition of the limits of skills, confidence, time and experience, it is possible to develop structures that enable discussion, input, and democratic decision-making. We don't want a top-down daycare system run by experts and professionals. Neither do we want to restrict involvement only to parents. We can collectively develop mechanisms to balance direct democratic power and to delegate aspects of control. Some of these innovative attempts to involve parents, staff, local people and local groups are outlined in the last chapter.

Margaret O'Brien Steinfels wrote: "No-one can say that women's liberation requires this or that particular kind or amount of daycare. It can be said that some new patterns of childcare are and will continue to be, a necessity."[10] In this

---

10. O'Brien Steinfels, M. 1972. *Who's Minding the children? The History and Politics of Daycare in America*. Simon and Schuster: New York. p. 246.

vision of childcare, we must be more honest about why we struggle to develop childcare services: not so much because they strengthen the family (for in doing that they also challenge much of what is wrong in the modern nuclear family), but because they improve the quality of people's lives and widen their choices.

Chapter Two

Children's Gifts

One thing about children we need to affirm at the start is that they come bearing gifts. This may seem too obvious for words. But the fact is so taken-for-granted, so widely overlooked, and yet so central to childcare that it must not only be stated but put at the centre of all that is said.

This is not the same as saying children are, themselves, gifts—an easy sentimental notion: "Ah yes, children are wonderful gifts—straight from the hand of God." The question soon becomes: "Now, what do we do with them?" And the formal public answer is to offer promises of an exalted status in society, appropriate to a god-like gift—promises that do not ring true to the actual, ambivalent position of children in the real world of adults, work and politics.

In fact, the vaunted status of children today parallels that of women in public esteem prior to 1950, when women—but especially stay-at-home mothers—were made out to be paragons of goodness and virtue who alone could keep the home safe from the wretchedness of the outside world. We can see now that this description of women smacked not only of adulation but control; the woman of the masculine dream was to stay on her pedestal so that the patriarchal world could unfold without women's interference.

Children seem caught in a similarly exclusionary definition. They are singled out as the prime objects of adult love, worthy of our finest care, and society's single best hope for the future.

But if we look closely at the status of children in our society, with even half a mind for honesty, we find an ominous underside to these platitudes. Here's how Germaine Greer puts it:

> "'Every child is a wanted child' is the slogan, but the modern Western infant is wanted by fewer people than any infants in our long history—not only fewer parents, but smaller groups of people.... Historically, human societies have been pro-child; modern society is unique in that it is profoundly hostile to children."[1]

To label children themselves as "gifts" obviates the gifts they bring to us and obscures the profound impact children have on adult lives, on the communities we live in, and on society itself. They come *bearing* gifts.

The point of gifts, and the probable reason why we fear to acknowledge and accept them, is the way they transform us. Ordinary market exchange does not have a similar capacity to affect the whole; it exists within the more abstract and instrumental realm of production and reproduction. But a gift exchange among human beings has the character of creating more than the sum of its parts.

Having so long tried to live by the admonition that "it is more blessed to give than to receive," we may have lost sight of the fact that receiving is part of the giving. Without acceptance the gift falls short and dies. The anthropologist Marcel Mauss, a scholar of gifts, offers an insight: He contended that gift economies were marked by three obligations: to give, to accept, and to reciprocate—that is, to give in return. Without all three of these activities taking place, people would be hurt, the gift circle destroyed, and the gift economy broken apart.

Two Human Economies

Lewis Hyde in his book, *The Gift*, points out that any work of art in our society exists in two economies at the same time: a gift economy and a market economy. Children also live in two economies. But the essential economy—the one that a child

---

1. Greer, G. 1984. *Sex and Destiny: The Politics of Human Fertility.* Harper and Row: New York. p. 2.

cannot long live without—is the gift economy. This gift-based society operates by laws other than those of the marketplace; it does not demand a "fair exchange," it does not bargain for a profit, it refuses to attach prices to what is given or received. It is a place of appreciation, growth and attachment, as opposed to depreciation, bargain-hunting and exclusion. Gifts given and received here rise in value as they are exchanged; they move people to extraordinary displays of prowess and gratitude.[2]

Of course the two economies are intertwined, and in most of life, the capitalist economy dominates. There is no escaping the capitalist economy of profit. Western societies have squelched the gift economy, pressed it into the tidy rituals of birthdays, Christmas exchanges and "charity." Yet within many homes and childcare situations there still do exist strong gift economies of mutuality and exchange. These places acknowledge the basic human need to give and receive without having to take account of one's self or to demand fair market value for what one gives.

As Hyde says, a gift economy has its boundaries. Outside it lies the exchange economy. People exist simultaneously in both economies, which are linked in fundamental ways. But the gift economy is fundamentally hostile to the market economy. Children who flourish in a gift economy need to learn to live within the economy of hard-nosed bargains and cut-throat competition. And to identify an intrusion of that system into the gift economy when they see one. And to defend what they love in both realms against disparagement.

Of course that larger market economy is no simple market. It is structured not only by competition and capitalism, but by class, racism and patriarchy and other elements that cut deeply into people's lives. In a world of oppression, segregation and competition, we can look to the gift economy to find resources. We can build on the strengths and weaknesses of our experiences at living in gift economies. And, part of the work of love, as the poet Adrienne Rich[3] says, is that it:

---

2. Hyde, L. 1979. *The Gift: Imagination and the Erotic Life of Property.* Vintage: New York.

3. "Natural Resources." 1978. In her *The Dream of a Common Language.* Norton: New York.

invents more merciful instruments
to touch the wound beyond the wound
does not faint with disgust
will not be driven off
keeps bearing witness calmly
against the predator, the parasite.

Love is no simple or easy thing. It demands of us that we work to change the world. That activity needs to be built on the fundamental understanding that adults need children as children need adults. We are in the truest sense peers.

A Union Of Love And Power

The understanding that children give as well as receive contains within it a democratic socialist vision of society and one in conflict with the capitalist market society. At the heart of this vision is a union of love and power: a person gives and receives out of trust and love, in a social environment of equality and justice. There should be no separation between the offering of one's truest strengths in society and the acceptance of that offering as a definitive part of society. That is to say, unless our gifts work to build society, we are consigned to live in a system of radical oppression. A basic part of the democratic socialist vision is that people's many and different gifts make a difference.

It follows from this that giving and receiving can only happen in community—a place where people face each other as equals who matter to each other. In the dominant world of exchange, where the many-levelled daily associations of life have been destroyed or abandoned, communities tend to be instrumental; people get together out of mutual interest or for particular causes—to fight a zoning change, get somebody elected to public office, start a softball league, or help each other take care of children. Each of these associations may be limited and partial, but they are an expression of community. These groupings may lack sustained associations, but their intensity of purpose can give social meaning and power to all persons involved.

A underlying assumption we work with is the conviction that children want to have a part in building a society rooted in the deepest and truest parts of themselves. Children, like adults, are actively engaged in building society. But this always happens within the contradictions of our present world. The child gradually discovers that things as she or he sees them are not entirely the way grown-ups say they are. What the child wants, and deems to be right and good, may not fit into the overall scheme of things for the family, school, mosque, or childcare centre. So the children's gifts meet a mixed reception. Yet children try to give against the odds, and in their particular ways; that's how they lay claim to their place in the human community. How can we express this core human activity that our children take part in from their earliest moments?

Small children are judged by their ability (or inability) to perform adult tasks. At seven, for example, a child can read the face of a non-digital clock. Much earlier, she learned to poo in a potty. At three a child could sort people according to sex. That's all true, but of course that's not a child. It seems an upside-down way, an "adult" way, of reading children. The achievements may be checkpoints on the way toward adulthood all right, but they seem hardly to show who a child is or what a child is about. It is like describing a train by telling how far it is from the station. True enough, life may be described as a series of developmental stages, but who is this person taking those stages, and what is he or she really trying to do in that process?

There are of course benefits in understanding the stages of a child's life. Child psychologist Jerome Kagan has shown brilliantly how children are often misunderstood by adults who misinterpret their abilities.[4] He points out, for example, that separation stress ebbs after two because children can begin to understand that an absent loved one will return. The child starts already at eight months, in fact, to be able to relate past to present and to predict the future. In other words, the child begins to gain a grasp on time, memory and prediction. It helps if adults know this, and think about the power of this dawning awareness.

But Kagan also points out that not all a child does—such as

---

4. Kagan, Jerome. 1984. *The Nature of the Child*. Basic Books: New York.

developing categories of concepts and schematizing reality—is necessarily in preparation for the future, although the child may be better prepared by doing it. A lot of it is just plain play. It's *being* rather than *becoming*. And children's play doesn't have to be about "producing," "performing," "improving" or "having"—even though many children are rushed into this busy-work. Children enrich their world by peopling it with imagination, and setting up situations to work through. This is mental acrobatics, pleasureful activity, a way of finding things out and making sense without having to make sense. Adults who impose a direction on this play ruin a good thing and add to children's deprivation.

In addition to their powers of mind, children have strong social impulses. Children are not simply candidates for socialization—the process by which children gain the habits, values, goals and knowledge that let them function as adults in society.[5] They are deeply social creatures, which means that socialization is not something that is simply done to them by others, but something they are actively engaged in themselves. It is essential to understand socialization as a lively childhood enterprise, self-motivated and outwardly direct, and aimed toward a contribution to the world the child has entered.

There is a delicate process which must be held in mind when we think about children. On the one hand, of course, children "absorb"—psychically, mentally, and physically—the culture in which they live. In this sense, they are the passive recipients of a culture which pre-dates them. But on the other hand, they create themselves and they change their culture. Children, like adults, constantly create and reconstitute themselves. A child's life is something like a complicated dance of self-creation and received socialization.

Yet each side of this inter-play is complex and contradictory. The process of embodying culture isn't a matter of simply being "socialized" by a single script. A child, just like an adult, must find her place in a complicated network of conflicting messages. When a young girl learns to be a "good girl," she learns a docility which probably won't let her be successful on

---

5. Maccoby, Eleanor E. 1980. *Social Development.* Harcourt Brace Jovanovich. p. v.

the corporate ladder. The moral directive of "do unto others" runs up against "don't let the bastards grind you down." Loving your family can be hard, when the "one-for-all" emphasis of the family squelches individuality. The complicated process of acculturation—received as well as self-created—occurs on the shifting and unstable ground of multiple discourses. The social world makes many conflicting demands which a child must somehow negotiate. Most of us recognize this intuitively, even if we can't explain it theoretically.

Self-creation, too, is far from a simple task. We want to be special and different, but we also want to belong. Sometimes we fight to be independent, and sometimes we're as dependent as babies. Between necessity and constraint, and a thousand impulses, we test ourselves through trial and error. There isn't a "pure me" waiting to unfold, the way a rose unfurls from a bud. The human task of self-creation is always dynamic. In a real sense, we don't so much "find" ourselves as we construct ourselves.

Most academic explanations of child development don't help us to understand this society/individual relation. When experts explain a child's psychological development, they overwhelmingly use an individualistic, liberal framework that denies the social component. When other experts try to explain the social component, they tend to underplay the individual and psychological aspect. In this chapter, we try to simultaneously explain both processes, although we place a heavy emphasis on the role of culture and politics. In part, this is a remedy against the common-sense belief that politics has nothing to do with children's development.

Building Trust

One of the things children do amid socialization is attempt to build trust, and at the same time learn to identify and deal with untrustworthy behaviour. Research is full of evidence showing how children react to situations where their efforts are accepted or spurned. An adult who constantly shouts at a seventeen-month-old "Don't do that" or "Leave that alone" or "Stop that" will turn out a child, on the average, who is timid, apathetic and joyless. And if that adult, on top of being harsh, shows little warmth toward the child, the child is likely to be withdrawn and hostile.

Further, the evidence shows that reasonable parents produce reasonable children. According to studies, parents who wield power arbitrarily and without explanation create children who are quiet, obedient and unassertive. Parents who guide children more democratically, with more talk and give-and-take, turn out children, on average, who are independent, competent, cheerful, self-controlled and socially responsible, with high self esteem.[6] Children actively work toward an accommodation with society that will let them add to it in a constructive way, when they are given a fair chance.

One person who most persuasively tried to think beyond a cookie-cutter notion of socialization in children was Erik Erikson. His book, *Childhood and Society*, published at mid-century, set out a series of psychosocial "crises" that a child must work through in growing up. Each of them is staged as an attempt to sort out some puzzling and often painful contradictions. The first of these is the tug of war between trust and mistrust. "The sense of trust," writes David Elkind, interpreting Erikson, "involves a feeling that the world is a safe place and that one's needs will be met. The sense of mistrust, on the other hand, involves the sense that the world is unsafe and unreliable, not trustworthy."[7]

There is first an awful, gnawing hunger in the belly, and then that warm intake of milk. There is, it seems, in an infant's fearfully vulnerable state, somebody out there to rely on. Yet once children have learned to fix their eyes on their mother's face and recognize her as the source of all that relief and joy, the mother leaves; she goes out of sight. Somehow, the child learns to deal with this conflict. When the child most needs her, she will return.

The child starts to trust those inner urges and desires. The rightness of that hunger is confirmed by the plenitude of that milk. Gradually the milk subsides as a basis for trust. It can be assumed. It is enveloped in an overall relationship that may

---

6. Maccoby, 1980, p. 386.

7. Elkind, D. 1987. *Miseducation: Preschoolers at Risk*. Knopf: New York. pp. 95–96.

include some partings and some returnings—but that is basically trustworthy.

"Parents," Erikson writes, "must not only have certain ways of guiding by prohibition and permission; they must also be able to represent to the child a deep, an almost somatic conviction that there is a meaning to what they are doing."[8] Not just mothers, but fathers too, are critical to child development. Struggles to come to terms with an absent, and hence untrustworthy, father can be equally informative in a child's development as her relationship with her mother.

We all know that both trust and mistrust are warranted in the world, but a child's starting to arrive at a workable resolution of that conflict depends on the child's first attachments. Reliable parents show the child what a solid response to the world can be like. But that knowledge is by no means merely intellectual: the whole being of the child responds to the messages coming back from that all-important person or persons, and the child's predisposition toward society gets its grounding in those first few months.

This is not to say a child with a good bonding to a loving adult will grow up without mistrust. Mistrust will be there, but it will assume a realistic place and later be directed at the proper targets. Untrustworthy behaviour will be identified over against the trust that has been established. The child will learn to mistrust aberrations; mistrust will not dominate the child's every thought and action.

A child's trust is a gift that can be abused; it demands responsibility by the adult. Elkind points out that premature physical, emotional or intellectual (terrifyingly, sometimes sexual) demands by adults can damage the child because the child trusts the adult so much and will, in turn, inflict those coercions on the self mercilessly. The child has to be able to grow in trust; the resolution will be a child who trusts the self.[9]

---

8. Erikson, Erik. 1963. *Childhood and Society*. 2nd ed. Norton: New York. p. 249.

9. This is the first but by no means the only crisis a child confronts. Others in the pre-school years are the attempt to attain self-control without the loss of self-esteem and the assertion of initiative in the face of guilt. That description oversimplifies Erikson's descriptions; they need to be read in the original.

Building Gender

Another thing a child struggles to work out is the matter of gender. Am I a girl or a boy, and what does that mean? It happens beneath conscious awareness. At one daycare centre one four-year-old said to another:

> "But I'm your boy friend."
> "I know that already," she replied. "Stop doing that."
> A moment later the boy said: "I'm not a boy."
> "Yes you are," she said.

Intimations of one's gender and what that means in the world of humans are built into the earliest relations between adults and child. Here is where sexism plays a crippling role.

An understanding of the imposition of patriarchy is necessary to envision what goes on with small children, and recent feminist thinking on the subject offers some valuable clues.

In Erikson's writing a child is always "he." One can partially explain his untroubled use of the masculine pronoun by remembering he wrote in the 1950s. If only it were as simple as getting the pronouns right! But patriarchy still clouded his findings, as it clouded his language. The problem was partly that it was not an issue, that it lay unchallenged in a "masculine" way of seeing and defining human reality. The patriarchal slant becomes clearer in Erikson's latter stages of childhood than in the earlier ones, but even there important factors were overlooked.

The unquestioned assumption that men's life pattern is the definitive human reality, with an aside for the female exception to the rule, is as old as the Genesis story of God shaping Eve out of Adam's rib. The use of men almost exclusively as the normative standard of human development puts a spin on things that only now is starting to be challenged. Oppressive gender scripts affected the work not just of Erikson, but of other students of child development including Sigmund Freud.[10]

Men have not only dominated and subdued women, but they have dominated and subdued those qualities which are associ-

---

10. Hancock, Emily. 1989. *The Girl Within*. Fawcett: New York. p. 229. "In taking the individual male's experience as his object of study and presuming the universality of what he found, Erikson carried forward a pattern set by Sigmund Freud."

ated with women. Both men and women have learned to devalue femininity (and women) and venerate masculinity (and men). Men learn to repress qualities associated with femininity in themselves and in actual women, and women take a complicated relationship to their own femininity. We not only come into the world with sexed bodies; we *learn* "female" and "male" because we live in a sexist world.

So how does that happen, and where does it start?

Recent work by feminist thinkers, notably Dorothy Dinnerstein and Nancy Chodorow, have pointed out the importance of the fact that, almost inevitably, a child's primary provider is a woman.[11] That is so ordinary as to be "normal and natural." But what is "normal and natural" has been made to be that way by human beings and has certain crucial effects.

Nancy Chodorow traces the gender conditioning of men and women to the different relationships between the boy or girl and the adult woman, who is almost always the dominant caregiver in infancy. That relationship of child to mother is shaped by the larger and unequal world of work and gender. Chodorow explains that a girl can experience herself as being essentially like her primary parent, identifying herself to herself in both the family and the world. A boy, on the other hand, feels he must break away from the maternal bond and identify himself with men, who are distant from the infant matrix. But since women are socially defined as inferior and less powerful, and men are socially defined as superior and worthy, positive identification with men and masculinity sets a psychic landscape that devalues women.

"Girls emerge from this period," she writes, "with a basis for 'empathy' built into their primary definition of self in a way that boys do not. Girls emerge with a stronger basis for experiencing another's needs or feelings as one's own...."[12] Boys, she says at another point, "come to define themselves as more separate and distinct, with a greater sense of rigid ego boundaries and differentiation. The basic feminine sense of

---

11. Chodorow, N. 1978. *The Reproduction of Mothering: Psychoanalysis and the Sociology of Gender.* University of California Press: Berkeley; Dinnerstein, D. 1977. The *Mermaid and the Minotaur: Sexual Arrangements and Human Malaise.* Harper Colophon: New York.

12. Chodorow, 1978, p. 167.

self is connected to the world, the basic masculine sense of self is separate."[13]

This basic gender identity—with masculinity achieved through separation and femininity achieved through attachment—is elaborated in the relationships of men and women throughout life. Other theorists have conjectured that it may explain in part why men have more trouble with human relationships, and women more trouble with "individuation" or standing independently of others. But it always means that we see each other, and ourselves, through the filter of gender. We can never avoid the omnipresence of gender. The "master script" of gender means that we're never simply a person: we're a *female* or a *male* person.

Chodorow asserts that the sexist splitting of women from men, and all the social consequences of power and oppression which accompany it, cannot be healed until both men and women assume early childcare. The fact that women give birth and breast-feed infants is no longer a reason to assign early care exclusively to women. If men took an equal part, the rigid definitions of gendered identity could give way to an integrated resolution of human potential.

Amy Rossiter, a social worker and researcher working at Families in Transition in Toronto, has carried Chodorow's analysis further.[14] Whereas Chodorow refutes the belief in biologism—that women's and men's biological differences in themselves consign them to different social roles—Rossiter also refuses the assumption that the special bond between mother and child should tie women to the roles prescribed by patriarchy.

In fact, Rossiter points out, mothers have to *learn* to care for children just as any parent would. Their closeness to infants may bond them to infants, but it doesn't have to bind them to patriarchal definitions of "Woman." It is patriarchal social construction of sexual differences, not the differences themselves, which account for the unequal imprisonment of women and men inside sexist categories.

---

13. Chodorow, 1978, p. 169.
14. Rossiter, A. 1988. *From Private to Public: A Feminist Exploration of Early Mothering.* Women's Press: Toronto.

Jessie Bernard points out that "The way we institutionalize motherhood in our society—assigning sole responsibility for childcare to the mother, cutting her off from the easy help of others in an isolated household, requiring round-the-clock tender, loving care, and making such care her exclusive activity—is new and unique."[15]

Amy Rossiter shows the debilitating toll of isolation on the life of a mother under the duress of her own love for an infant. "Such work," she writes, "requires a tremendous fluidity of identity: suspending one's own identity to be the baby in order to understand her needs, dissolving one's boundaries to admit a different rhythm, thinking with a constant sub-thought of 'baby'... in conditions of isolation this fluidity is experienced as a loss of self—not because babies are so voracious, but because the social institutions in which one's identity is normally constituted simply disappear. Mothers are left without the social interactions which construct and produce identity; at the same time, they are expected to perform work which demands a kind of diffusion of identity. In a very real sense, mothers feel they have 'lost' their selves."[16]

Small wonder that mothers have conflicted and ambivalent feelings. A mother requires, as Rossiter says, "a peopled landscape" in which to revive and reconfirm her sense of self and identity precisely in order that she can do good by the child.[17] Germaine Greer points out that "the best mother in the world cannot continue for long on a diet of dreary routine chores and insatiable infant demand: if she is not to suffer from serious psychic deprivation she must have stimulation and communication with supportive peers, as well as rest."[18]

Sexist family structures mean that women's labour of mothering is undertaken in the service of patriarchy. "These practices have been overlaid on maternal-infant attachment for so long that we have come to understand that attachment, based in biology, as necessitating a particular form of mothering

---

15. Bernard, Jessie. 1975. *The Future of Motherhood*. Penguin: London. p. 9.
16. Rossiter, 1988. p. 244.
17. Rossiter, 1988. p. 248.
18. Greer, German. 1984. *Sex and Destiny: The Politics of Human Fertility*. Picador: London. p. 13.

called 'staying at home.' We have lost the actual history of women's separation from the workplace, while the social arrangements of mothering are made to seem the 'natural and normal' outcome of attachment."[19] The problem lies in patriarchal norms, not in the special attachment of infants to mothers. Men do need to be fully involved with children but that alone won't undo the problem of male power and privilege and female subordination. The elimination of patriarchy and gender itself is what is required, not merely a "kinder, gentler" sex-role distribution.

We cannot fully imagine what it might mean to live in a sexed body without social prescriptions for gender. We cannot predict how our personal identity would be organized, how erotic desire might change, how we might form intimate relationships differently, or organize our families—or even what childcare might mean in a world beyond sexual and gender organization. But this is the perspective that we need to hold in mind as we consider alternative ways to care for children.

Building The Self

The difficulties in building trust and gender are by no means the only conflicts which children must tackle. The struggle to build a sense of self is a life-long project, in which childhood roots are absolutely critical. This project of self-construction occurs at both conscious and unconscious levels. Simple sociological theories of socialization leave the unconscious dimensions of this struggle untouched. To understand how building a sense of self involves unconscious and preconscious dynamics demands we turn to psychoanalysis. For all of the troubling prejudices and conservatism of Freudian thought, it offers us a way to think about our deepest selves.

A particular gift of psychoanalysis, within which Chodorow couches her insight, is to recognize the presence and power of the human unconscious. Children as they work things out develop a self that accommodates to the world by both accepting it and denying it—and this relates to unconscious realities.

As Eleanor Maccoby points out in her book, *Social Development*, social scientists often find psychoanalytic claims diffi-

---

19. Rossiter, 1988. p. 15.

cult to prove. And yet those claims provide a useful antidote to the flat, often desocialised behavioural approach to children that is inclined to destroy the whole by studying the isolated parts.

A psychiatrist, Harry Stack Sullivan, once gave a simple description of the child's self-sorting activity as being one of dividing the self into a few categories. One part is a "good me," which is what the child usually refers to when saying "I." Accumulated in the "good me" are all the things about the child that adults look upon fondly. Then there's the "bad me," of which adults disapprove, but which still may form a part of the child's conscious sense of self. And finally there's the "not me," organized by the things adults fear or hold in revulsion, from hurting a sibling to eating feces. Sullivan contended that most children have a set of "uncanny emotions," including awe, horror, loathing or dread, under which they hide from themselves certain desires or attributes. That's the "not me," and a part of the reservoir of the unconscious. Part of the "not me" is what boys learn to do with things labelled "girl" and vice versa—one example of the repression principle at work. This is partly why gender goes so deep: it, like other social identities, organizes our most basic interior landscape.

Young children are separated from the rest of humanity by a great forgetting. Those early stages of infancy, so hugely filled with hungers, fears, angers and delights, but so blanketed too with the rage of helplessness, is a world soon relegated by a growing child to the world of "not-me." The memory may still work at unconscious levels as a constant unacknowledged longing—to be helpless, to be encradled, to be breast-fed in a blissful nirvana—but it is a world soon surpassed and consciously disowned. The child wants self control, significance and place.

What have we all left behind in that reservoir of forgetting? There is an immense physicality of being a child, the joy of having dexterous arms and legs, the delight of shitting, the feel of a hot-wet diaper and a cold-soggy one, the amazing power of first turning over in bed. The startling fact that doorways take people away and bring people back. Being able to crawl, walk, and push open a door. The terror of being left alone, the angry-joyful pangs of being reunited. Child care requires, among other things, the imagination to wonder what life is really like for young children.

Far from being powerless, children have mindful bodies with which to experience the world, process its raw materials, and come up with questions and answers. At the same time, as we have seen, much of what they give cannot be received in the society as it now is. The basic questions of goodness and evil in society afflict them to the core, as they do anybody else. Even their "thinking skills" tend to be regulated and placed at the service of a market economy as if that were all there was. To stay in touch with the gift economy is a continuing problem of a child's life. Children need adults around them who not only acknowledge this struggle but put up a fight of their own.

Recent research findings into children's thinking powers show us that the capacity of children to reason and work toward a constructive understanding of the world has been underrated by psychologists in the past. Far from being the "buzzing, booming confusion" it was thought to be, early infancy is a time of intense perception and learning. Not only that, but an infant, according to psychologist T. G. R. Bowers, perceives itself as a member of the human race right from the start, displaying amazing powers of recognition and identity between itself and the people taking care of it. For instance, a six-day-old baby can already imitate its mother when she sticks out her tongue, Bowers observed. "The baby recognizes that his own tongue, which he can only know by the feel of it in his mouth and between his lips, matches his mother's tongue, which he sees—and this is truly astonishing."[20]

It was once thought that infants acted only in response to rewards, that they learned only to get things to assuage basic "drives" such as thirst and hunger. But researcher Hanus Papousek did a series of studies showing that's just not true: children learn to do a whole lot of things for the mere satisfaction and joy of doing them. Papousek reasoned from his experiments with infants that they show, in the words of Margaret Donaldson, "a fundamental human urge to make sense of the

---

20. Bowers, T.G.R. 1977. *The Perceptual World of the Child*. Harvard University Press: Cambridge, Mass. p. 28.

world and bring it under deliberate control."[21] They are judging their encounters with the world by some kind of internal "standard" that they will build into a model of what the whole is like.

Even the Piagetian notion that intelligence in a child under seven is very restricted has been roundly rebutted. One of the reasons for Jean Piaget's finding in the first place was a fairly restricted set of tests that he and his followers had set up to find out how children think. One of Piaget's central tests found young children unable to "decentre" in their thinking.[22] That is, they were judged to be unable to imagine a situation from another's point of view.[23] In the 1970s, it was discovered that the interpretations of the earlier tests by Piaget's followers had been too narrowly conceived. It turned out to be the adult researchers who had not been able to "decentre" adequately so as to imagine the situation of the child. In fact, the children showed far greater powers of varied and imaginative thinking than had been previously recognized.

Margaret Donaldson suggests that the young child not only questions the world at a very early age—probably before learning to talk—but also wants to think in some way beyond it. "These questionings and these strivings," she writes, "imply some primitive sense of possibility which reaches beyond a realization of how things are to a realization of how they might be."[25]

When it comes to learning, Donaldson finds people, including children, to be far from the reactive agents that many researchers have taken them for. "We do not just sit and wait for the world to impinge on us," she writes of both children and adults. "We try actively to interpret it, to make sense of it. We grapple with it, we construe it intellectually, we represent it to ourselves."[26] She and others revealed through painstaking experiments with children that what child researchers before took to be disabilities turn out rather to have been adult inabili-

---

21. Donaldson, M. 1978. *Children's Minds*. Norton: New York. p. 116.
22. Donaldson, 1978, p. 13–17.
23. Donaldson, 1978, p. 90.
25. Donaldson, 1978, p. 87.
26. Donaldson, 1978, p. 67.

ties to understand the levels of value at which children were thinking.

It seems to have taken a long time for child psychologists to imagine the reality of children's thinking, that is, to receive what children give, rather than to extrapolate their way of thought from adult—and system-clad—notions of thinking.[27]

Building A Society

At the same time as children are building a self, they are helping to build a society. They are an integral part, at first, of small, intimate "societies" known as homes, usually organised by the nuclear family. Although the nuclear heterosexual family is considered the norm—what we (incorrectly) think is average and normal—it is only one way of having a "family". The real question is: how can we extend the ways that adults and children can live together, in loving, caring and growing relationships—at both the personal and the social level?

Children are multi-layered people, as we all are. A child doesn't come into the world the way behaviourist John Watson described it as a mere "squirming bit of flesh," but as an intricate being with certain ready-made aptitudes and abilities, and a distinct temperament. This incipient personality relates to its family initially with all it has; it holds nothing back. This all-out investment puts it, of course, at the mercy of its environment, but it doesn't soak up that environment like an ink blotter; it tries from the very start to "make sense" of it, to figure it out, to grasp the edges of the shape of the world it has been plopped into the middle of, and to tailor itself along certain findings. That's the start of socialization and also the building of society.

This makes the "family"—the nest of the child's first formulations—essential to the delicate checks and balances that a

---

[27]. Mary Catherine Bateson shows an understanding of this in her book, *Composing a Life* (1989. Atlantic Monthly Press: New York. p. 107)—
"Although children are small and physically helpless, their capacity for rapid learning and problem solving is impressive—it is just that the adult carries around a fund of learned solutions. Children might be better off if parents were more aware of themselves as learning from them, rejuvenated by them, and ultimately perhaps dependent upon them."

child incorporates in growing up. The centrality of this environment in a child's life makes the individual in some ways indescribable outside of intimate relationships. Theorists have asked the question: Can persons as we know them exist without family? How essential to autonomous individuals are family structures?

Such nagging questions have caused some social critics to assume—or at least debate—whether or not childcare outside the home causes damage to children's development. That was part of Bruno Bettelheim's quest when he visited the Israeli kibbutzim in 1964 and wrote about their communal child-rearing in *The Children of the Dream*. He found that children raised outside of nuclear families were different. In the collective child-rearing of the kibbutzim they tended to become more outwardly directed, more group oriented, less anxiety-ridden and more secure. Their personalities were less individuated than American children in nuclear families which Bettelheim had also studied. "These children of theirs," he concluded, "are not the stuff dreams are made of, but real people at home since their birth, on native ground."[28] His study did confirm the broad proposition that early childcare—whether in a privatised or collective "family"—does have profound implications for the personalities of those within it—personalities raised in active relationships with intimate and not so intimate others.

Another book by Bettelheim, *The Uses of Enchantment*, is an inquiry into fairy tales in the lives of children. Here he also deals with family, but extends his concern to forces which are much broader and more terrifying. Bettelheim offers fairy tales as an introduction for the child to a deep moral order that undergirds society. Children can see in these tales the social forces that they intuit in their parents and that they discern dimly beyond the horizon of their homes.

At this time in history our children live in a society where forces of class oppression, racism, sexism and imperialism militate against a loving social order. The gift economy is fragile in comparison to the capitalist market economy, and children's attempts to work out a relationship between the two can

---

28. Bettelheim, B. 1973. *Children of the Dream*. Paladin: New York. p. 283.

be enormously instructive. This is evident in small and large things, but none of them small to the child. What does it mean when a child of three flees in terror from a TV commercial that shows a terrible giant breaking open a doll? How do children respond when they see others singled out and punished for having talked at nap-time? Their reactions may be full of conflict, but they bring questions of right and wrong to the picture that adults need to recognize and support.

But the market economy impinges on childhood so powerfully that one has to wonder whether their own recognitions have a chance to emerge. Canadian children between the ages of two to six watch television an average of 20 hours a week. That constitutes, in the words of sociologist Margrit Eichler, "an extraordinarily important factor in the lives of children."[29] And she characterizes the programming they get as overwhelmingly "American-dominated, sexist, violent and consumer-oriented."[30]

Twenty hours a week—that's only the average—is more than a child is likely to spend at mealtimes the whole week, and most likely far more than a child ever spends relating to any adult aside from a tired, overworked mother. Perhaps talk of the threatened dissolution of the family environment is a moot point. Perhaps it already happened in the 1950's and 60's along with the coming of TV. "As watching television replaces all other social rituals," writes social critic Joyce Nelson, "it becomes the unacknowledged ritual container: triggering archetypal responses and naming them with the brand names, consumer mores, celebrity faces and catch-phrases of the marketplace. These TV mediations become what we have in common."[31] Television, in fact, offers a talking point for getting children out of the home and into daycare, where at least most of their association will be with live people—who can breath, see, hear, react and respond.

Television, of course, is only one window on the wider world. But it presents a fair array of the forces at work outside

---

29. Eichler, M. 1988. *Families in Canada.* Today. 2nd ed. Gage: Toronto. p. 334.
30. Eichler, M. 1988, p. 336.
31. Nelson, J. 1987. *The Perfect Machine.* Between the Lines: Toronto. p. 77.

the home that aim to undermine the gift economy with the larger imperatives of commercial values and capital accumulation. Its mediations leave pointedly "unmediated," that is, outside of separate evaluation and judgment, the demands that it places on people victimized by its spell, as children often are.

Building Social Class

More children live in poverty than do the members of any other age group in Canada. (This will be spelled out in greater detail in Chapter Four.) Children in our society suffer not just the allures, but also the brunt, of market-place logic. The reason for this is a dogged reliance on capitalist economics to organise social life. Children's welfare (like everyone else's) has been left largely to the market economy; the well-being of children in Canada rides on the highs and lows of national and international commerce and is secondary to the private accumulation of capital. So when bad times come we are told by capitalist economics that there is little to be done but try to last it out—while children, like adults, suffer the effects.

There is more to poverty than meets the eye, but little of it escapes the child. Eleanor Maccoby points out in *Social Development* that a child's first social mirror is the eyes of the parent. What the child sees in that mirror is the child's first civic lesson. The child reads her own worth or lack of worth; detects whether the world is just, equitable and humane; picks up either the hurt or the joy in one's own lot in life. A parent who is harried, manipulated or exploited may be a great parent, but the truth of that person's social status in the world also registers on the soul of the child. Like as not, the child takes the blame for the trouble. In working class, visible minority, and other marginalized families, children usually internalize the social judgment. Thus begins what sociologists call the cycle of poverty and self-oppression—aside from whatever hardships and indignities the child will suffer later.

In a kind of a reverse way, this explains the often buoyant ego of the child in a privileged family. For children whose parents enjoy social power and prestige, there is a spill-over acquisition of confidence and a sense of entitlement. These children are convinced that all good things will come to them, and that such gifts are their due. In this environment, children—like their parents—can come to believe that their good fortune is their own personal accomplishment.

In liberal and middle class families, there is usually a myth that systemic power has not shaped their lives. In truth, of course, we are all born into a place in a social, sexual, and racial hierarchy. Each of us is affected by the accidents of our birth. While we have some room to change the social path which was laid out for us at birth, these larger forces will never be entirely overcome.

Michael Lerner, a psychotherapist, social activist and recently, editor of the magazine *Tikkun*, acknowledges poverty as a source of great grief to children, but he sees the larger world of work, as it has been organized by capitalism, to be a wrecker of family life and the life of the child whether or not embedded in poverty. "The child discovers itself in the eyes of its parents," he writes, "but most parents do not really see the child."[32] He points out that parents who suffer the indignities of class and alienating work often bring home a blindness to children that damages the home environment. This is not to be blamed exclusively on parents. They most often cope as best they can, and they try to love their children well. This love is something most children experience deeply, even though it is often only unconsciously acknowledged or expressed, and it stirs in them the hope upon which to build their lives. "But it is also important to see," Lerner writes, "that the general picture is that most parents, despite all the love they feel for their children, are so absorbed in the emotional pains inflicted by the world of work, the frustrated hopes of compensation in family life, and the legacies of their own childhoods, that they cannot give the spontaneous love and recognition that their children need."[33]

Beneath all this, and running through it, are the impositions of class. That hidden spoiler cannot be discounted simply because class divisions in North America are sometimes permeable, allowing some to "rise above" their class—and in this

---

32. Lerner, M. 1986. *Surplus Powerlessness*. The Institute of Labour and Mental Health: Oakland, California. p. 126.

33. Lerner, 1986, p. 129.

way promotes the myth that class depends on individual merit and hard work. As Richard Sennett and Jonathan Cobb have shown in *The Hidden Injuries of Class*, the poor often fall victim to a "logic of discontent" that sets child against child instead of directing children's frustration and anger at the true sources of oppression, which is the logic of capitalism itself. Sennett and Cobb show how this starts in school and how it follows the working-class child throughout life. An ideology of individualism—asserting that being working class is a personal fault and a failure—delegitimizes valid grievances and works against struggles to challenge class relations.

Middle class experts often judge working class families to be defective. Those same middle class experts rarely can recognize the way their own class expectations affect their children. In the name of "improving" children, middle-class adults also often tamper with them. Children's activities are part of the display of class-appropriateness. Children are to give evidence of their cultural capital: Their toys are "educational."[34] They are encouraged to practice "discipline." They are hurried along in their growing up. Their sports/musical/creative skills are evidence of their families' class. This is a different kind of adult presence than in working-class families, but it is still the imposition of class.

Building Culture

What is true of social class is true of other unwanted cultural impositions on the child—those of racism, sexism, the conflicting demands of jingoism and patriotism, and the threats of global war and environmental ruin. These influences bear on children from earliest consciousness. But while they make their demands on children, children also fight back. The point is to recognize the struggle that a child makes at whatever level to create a world that makes sense, and that enables people to build love, dignity and equality.

This takes a sense of citizenship on the part of adults: a

---

34. Bourdieu, P. 1984. *Distinction: A Social Critique of the Judgement of Taste*. Harvard University Press: Cambridge. See also Walkerdine, V. and H. Lucey. 1989. *Democracy in the Kitchen: Regulating Mothers and Socializing Daughters*. Verso: London.

vision, as Ken Osborne describes it in *Educating Citizens*, "of the good society as a cooperative commonwealth, in which all citizens work equally together for the common good."[35] This is a collective, not a privatised, vision. Diverse and multiple families and family forms which are strongly linked to social life, not an escape from society, are a key component of that vision.

Along with this, there needs to be a justified pride in the progress we have made so far in building Canada as a nation—its incorporation of "two nations" in a single state, its multiculturalism and hospitality to refugees, its decent health-care systems, its livable cities, its workable Crown corporations (especially in transportation and media but also in industry) and its initiatives in working for a peaceful world order, to name a few.

These accomplishments stand there too for children to observe, join and strengthen. They stand against the racism, sexism and jingoism that children must also confront. Patriotism need not be the last refuge of a scoundrel: it can be based on pride at the ways we have worked to build a caring society.

This social vision is rooted partly in the progressive side of rural and small-town life that persisted in Canada as a powerful reality well into the middle of the 20th century. And it exists partly in the links of a strong minority of Canadians to socialism and trade unionism, to feminism, to the liberation of people of colour, and to other new social movements committed to quality-of-life issues. As Gad Horowitz points out in *Canadian Labour in Politics*, it was the old Canadian Congress of Labour, and then the New Democratic Party, that typically proposed the social reforms that the Tories or the Liberals eventually found themselves able to put in place. Canadian politics have been decisively different from those of the United States because Canada has a much stronger democratic socialist tradition—though one that is under massive attack.

What our children will do with all this is all our business. We can make their care an extension of the best of our desire

---

35. Osborne, K. 1988. *Educating Citizens: A Democratic Socialist Agenda for Canadian Education*. Our Schools/Our Selves: Toronto. p. 5.

and struggles for a caring and just society. That at least will offer them something with which they can join forces and will create an environment open to their efforts. This awareness is a basis for insisting that childcare be "in community"—not a mere part of a "welfare/service" system—and it provides the basis for developing a national childcare programme, which will be discussed later.

But to set the stage for such proposals we need to see what has happened to families and communities in our past, how they have cared for children, and what endures in those institutions that we can build on for the future.

Chapter Three

Family and Home

The Meaning Of Family

A public policy of community childcare can be built out of our experiences of the strengths and struggles of family and home. But to do this we have to look at the history of families and question the meanings of home. When we look beneath common-sense, we find that the definition, meaning and practices of families have varied widely.

Feminists have contributed much to our understanding of the history and changing practices of families. One of their most significant contributions has been to point out that "the family" is not only an institution but a set of ideas—which are "prescriptive" even more than they are descriptive of actual families. The concept of "the family" has an important ideological role: its power comes from the way we make "families" an organizing principle of social policy and social life.

"Family," as an ideology, exists mainly in symbolic opposition to what it isn't: to the market, civil society, or the state. In this respect, family is a uniquely modern institution.[1] The concept of "family" as a distinct domain from the rest of life only happened when modern life became organized around capital-

---

1. Collier, J, M. Rosald and S. Yanagisko. 1982. "Is There a Family? New Anthropological Views." In (Eds.) B. Thorne and M. Yalom. *Rethinking the Family*. Longman: New York and London. pp. 25–39.

ist enterprise. Before the transition away from feudalism to capitalism, families were linked in a web of inter-connected relations—where work and home were often the same place and involved the same people. In many parts of the world, this is still the case.

Yet popular wisdom assumes "the family," as opposed to the actual families we live in, is universal, monolithic, and ahistorical. This is opposed by new research which suggests that no specific family arrangement is natural, biological, or "functional" in a timeless way. While the birthing of children by women is an undeniable biological fact, the arrangements of child-rearing are equally undeniably *social*. In different cultures, societies have developed a variety of institutions to manage the labour of childcare.

Our current North American assumptions about the role of mothering are not borne out by cross-cultural comparative work.[2] In one study listed in the anthropological Human Relations Area Files, caretaking patterns in 186 different cultures were examined.[3] In only 46% were biological mothers the primary caretakers of infants. In four-fifths, someone other than the biological mother was the primary caretaker of children after infancy. One anthropologist argues that care of several young children by one or more adults has a "many times longer human history" than exclusive mother-child relationships.[4]

In fact, some anthropologists have argued that: "Tribal people may speak readily of lineages, households, and clans, but—as we have seen—they rarely have a word denoting 'Family' as a particular and limited group of kin; they rarely worry about differences between legitimate and illegitimate heirs or find themselves concerned (as we so often are today) that what children and/or parents do reflects on their family's public image and self-esteem."[5] In societies without a public/private distinction or market relations, the meaning of

---

2. Collier, et al, 1982.

3. Margolis, M. 1985. *Mothers and Such: American Women and Why They Changed.* University of California Press: Berkley. p.15.

4. Chodorow, N. 1978. *The Reproduction of Mothering.* University of California Press: Berkley. p. 74.

5. Collier, et al, p. 32.

family is radically different than ours.

This critical insight rejects common-sense ideas about the naturalness of the isolated family.[6] In fact, the family that emerges from recent feminist scholarship is infinitely varied. We should talk about "families" instead of "the family." Researchers warn that whenever the family is talked about as "natural," we should become suspicious.[7]

Studying families as they actually exist turns up a host of issues, including heterosexism, child-rearing patterns, motherhood, the sexual division of labour, and family-state interactions. And families are found to be very different for women than for men. Men may think of them as "havens" from the outside world, but for women they are sites of never-ending work (which women could have told researchers years ago). Not only that, families are often dangerous and violent places for women and children. Behind closed doors, in a "man's castle," much unjust behavior has gone unseen and unchallenged.

Another finding is that the boundaries between families and the outside world are not the clear-cut demarcation lines of the popular, scholarly or bureaucratic imagination. The great divide between the private-family and the public-state is a powerful idea, but seen close up it often scarcely seems to exist. Families share the larger social, economic and political crises of the larger society.[8] The problems of the family are a microcosm of the contradictions of our contemporary society.

It is a wistful notion to valorize "the family" as a last refuge from impersonal, alienated and commodified market forces. Yet this valorization of "the family" is at one and the same time both reactionary and progressive. It is reactionary when it reinforces, as the New Right tries to do, the most oppressive features of the patriarchal and monolithic family. But it is progressive when it catches hold of something that is of real worth and has been preserved, in however a damaged form, by way of human intimacy and close, enduring personal ties.

---

6. Barrett, M. and M. McIntosh. 1982. *The Anti-Social Family.* Verso: London.

7. Collier, et al, p. 57.

8. See the excellent review article by Barry Thorne. In (Eds.) B. Thorne and M. Yalom. 1982. *Rethinking the Family.* Longman: New York and London.

It takes careful critical thinking to see through the ideological use of "the family." It takes discernment as well to see— not to give up on—the ideals of nurture and care that stand at the heart of what we want families to do. Beyond the myth of "the family" are those diverse and complicated households and human relationships that we find ourselves living in. Real families are a complex mix of love and violence, oppression and support, for adults and children.

Challenges to "the family" are difficult to hear because they are seen as attacks on the most comforting and vital human relationships we know. Eli Zaretsky has said that: "It is a tragic paradox that the bases of love, dependence and altruism in human life and the historical oppression of women have been found within the same matrix."[9] But we can't built families that really support their members if we are unwilling to face the ways families have changed historically and have been shaped by their internal relations as well as market forces and public policy.

Looking At Canadian Families

What about families in Canada? They may have changed more in the past twenty years than in the previous seventy, as sociologists say that they have, but the long view requires going back at least to the middle of the past century when families were quite different from today. So were the schools, and so was society, as was the organization of work, the economy and the state. It takes an awareness of this to appreciate the choices we face with children today.[10]

For one thing, Canadian society at that time had not yet moved into the major social classes that exist today. There were certainly the self-conscious gentry, the big land-owners, and the political elite. In Upper Canada, for example, the Family Compact clearly held a monopoly on centralized power. Ordinary people—mostly farmers and craftsmen—often saw

---

9. Zaretsky, E. 1982. "Family and the Origins of the Welfare State." In (Eds.) B. Thorne and M. Yalom. *Rethinking the Family*. Longman: New York and London. p. 193.

10. This review is based on the experience of Upper Canada: other English-speaking provinces developed along similar lines.

themselves belonging to particular stations of life. As historian Alison Prentice describes mid-19th Century society, its members were part of a fixed social hierarchy with ranks and orders that were mutually dependent and not in strong competition. Prior to 1850, a leading Upper Canadian schoolman, Bishop John Strachan, described these fixed ranks and orders as fitting and proper; he said that a man who "got above himself" was bound to suffer envy, melancholy, hatred and chagrin.[11] This view was that of a member of the Compact and not totally shared, but it expressed a common sentiment; social mobility was not then a universal goal.

There was also a solidarity among farmers and artisan/tradesmen of that time. As late as 1850 they still made up the majority of the occupations in Canada West.[12] The strength of these allied occupational groups, buoyed up by the easy availability of good farmland, slowed the rise of industrial capitalism in Canada, and formed the basis for the Farmer's Revolt of 1837 as well as the formation of the Farmer/Labour Party after World War I. Among these people, along with the view of "fixed stations in life," was a consciousness of themselves as a class of independent producers, and this included an understanding of class enemies among the merchant ruling class. There certainly were differences in wealth among the farmer/artisan majority, but there was also a substantial social equality among these independent producers; there were only a few steps in the social hierarchy to be conscious of on a daily basis; the majority of the people saw themselves in much the same class, living together in villages and rural communities.

The work they did was locally based; it took place in and around the household and the farm. Families were people who worked together, not just lived together. And families were much bigger than a nuclear husband and wife and their chil-

---

11. Prentice, A. 1977. *The School Promoters*. McClelland and Stewart: Toronto. p. 91.

12. Johnson, Leo A. April, 1981. "Independent Commodity Production: Mode of Production or Capitalist Class Formation?" *Studies in Political Economy*. No. 6, p. 107. As William Lyon Mackenzie wrote in 1834: "The farmer toils, the merchant toils, the labourer toils, and the Family Compact reap the fruit of their exertions." Quoted by Stanley Ryerson, in *Unequal Union*, 1968. International Publishers: New York. p. 93.

dren: they included relatives, servants, boarders and friends. Men were farmers, fishermen, blacksmiths and merchants who most often worked from their homes or in small teams. Women were much more than just the bearers and rearers of children. They cared for the household—spinning, weaving, soap-making, preserving food and so on—and their direct labour kept the family alive and able to be productive. The household was largely self sufficient, and women—though subservient to men—were as much a part of that self-sufficiency as men were.[13] Households and families were situated in larger geographic communities that influenced the family. The family was a key, interactive part of the social order that surrounded it.

The place of children was clearly defined. Daughters joined their mothers in the work of the household; sons frequently followed the trades of their fathers. Each child counted as a producer. Children, in fact, performed essential tasks; without children working on the farm, a family simply could not survive.[14] Children understood they were needed in the whole operation even as the whole contributed to their long-range survival. One of the sons would eventually run the family farm or trade. There was a sense of carrying on the ordering of society through families.

Local governments were based on the township and the school section and rooted in the economic, social and political communities of farm families. During the first half of the 19th century, they were in a fierce tug-of-war with the central provincial government. Within this agrarian society was a traditional notion of egalitarianism based roughly on equal family ownership of land. Its people struggled hard to hold on to local control of their communities. Many of their egalitarian values are still powerful today if mainly in opposition to the dominant—and now urban—centralized political and corporate powers.

---

13. See Illich, Ivan. 1981. *Shadow Work*. Marion Boyars: Boston, p. 111–12, for a short description of the devolution in Western society of the family from a production to a consumption unit, and the effects of this on women's work.

14. Children are capable of meaningful and productive work. It is an historical anomoly that contemporary practices and current common-sense do not recognize this productivity in both families and childcare programmes.

Changes Of Industrial Capitalism

At mid-century in Canada West (now Ontario)—earlier than that in other parts of the Western world—industrialization began to change the economic and political reality of families. The changes came gradually but surely with the amassing of capital. They took a century to complete, but by the end the social order was profoundly altered by new forms of social and political control. Men began taking wage-jobs in factories and losing ownership and control of their farms and shops. Women no longer managed productive households and became "housewives"—doers of chores, care-takers of children and comforters of husbands.

Many farms started turning into commercial operations, precursors to the agribusiness enterprises of the latter 20th century. What had been a farming and a local resource-based economy, centred in small villages and towns, was turned into a modern, if colonized, industrial nation under centralized corporate control. An industrial society eclipsed the older rural one.

Along with industrialization came the break up of traditional status and rank and the old class structure. The notion of society "as a multi-levelled, hierarchical and rather static structure of interdependent ranks" gave way to "the idea that increasingly the community was made up of two great classes only," writes historian Alison Prentice.[15] Those two classes were to be the labouring poor and the middle class, dominated by a small elite.

As women and men moved into new roles created by these changes—sometimes reluctantly, sometimes with gusto—the family changed. Now, instead of being self-sufficient in producing and consuming, it produced less and consumed more. The husband's job was bringing home the cash, and the task of the wife, as Ivan Illich puts it, "became the organization of compulsory consumption"; he calls it the beginning of "shadow work"—the labour that does not receive pay but which is essential to industrial production.[16] Women's shadow work

---

15. Prentice, 1977. p. 67.
16. Illich, I. 1981. *Shadow Work*. Marion Boyars: Boston. p. 112.

was the labour of consumption. Being an actively working consumer was, and is, vitally important. A great deal of invisible labour is required to transform a pay package into cooked meals, clean clothes, and a liveable household. A household organized around money—or the lack of it—needs someone to do consumer work in a way that a directly productive family doesn't.

Some Early Protests

Women variously embraced and rejected the notion of compulsory motherhood. Early feminist reformers during the early part of the 19th century advocated "voluntary motherhood," a movement which Linda Gordon calls "motherhood writ large."[17] By celebrating women's supposed natural attributes of nurturance and caretaking, the idea of "social housekeeping" emerged—a kind of mothers for the nation.

This provided a rationale for a distinctly female (if not feminist) voice in political and social affairs. The Voluntary Motherhood movement often couched demands for greater respect for women in the language of greater respect for motherhood. Although they did not challenge assumptions about the family or of the sexual division of labour, they wanted their separate sphere to be socially validated.

In 1850, Charlotte Perkins Gilman argued, as she had for over five decades, that "women must create feminist homes with socialized housework and childcare before they could become truly equal members of society."[18]

But these radical critiques fell on hard times. Primary female caretaking of children is now so much a part of normal female identity that its social organizaton has become invisible. Because invisible, it seems natural and spontaneous. In the absence of an analysis of parenting, primary mother-care

---

17. Gordon, L. 1982. "Why 19th century feminists didn't support 'birth control' and 20th century feminists do.": Feminism, reproduction and the family." In (Eds.) B. Thorne and M. Yalom. *Rethinking the Family.* Longman: New York.

18. Cited in Caroline New and Miriam David. 1985. *For the Children's Sake: Making Childcare More Than Women's Business.* Penguin: London. p. 15.

became internalized by mothers (and fathers) as normal, experienced by society as "natural," and then became the basis for social policy.

Maxine Margolis notes that in 18th century America, prescriptive advice about parenting—except for what came from ministers and priests—did not exist.[19] In the late 19th century, child development gradually came to be viewed as the major, if not sole, responsibility of mothers. They were urged to devote themselves full-time to parenting duties. A storm of experts' books, prescriptive suggestions, and market advice-giving arose as a result. Margolis' fascinating survey of the historical changes introduced in the advice books through war, depression, recession, inflation and social change provide an illuminating glimpse of the constructions of what has since been taken to be a "natural" unit—the family.

Centralized School Control

With the industrial revolution came the control of public schooling by the central government. In Ontario a half century of conflict between farm-based communities and centralist, urban-oriented "school promoters" resulted in the School Act of 1871. This act established universal, state-financed, compulsory schooling for all Ontario children. A simular logic operated throughout the rest of the provinces.

As historians Alison Prentice and Bruce Curtis have both pointed out, a centrally controlled public school system did not arise out of popular demand. It came largely out of the need to transform rural children into industrial workers. The blessings of middle-class sensibilities and ways of conduct were to be spread to the lower classes without necessarily improving their station in life. The aim was the internal peace of society.

Prentice says schooling was organized to accomplish a certain kind of social harmony: "Class conflict would be eliminated, in other words, by getting the lower classes to take on the values of the higher." She quotes Egerton Ryerson, who founded the school system of Canada West: "It is clearly within the

---

19. Margolis, M. 1985.

province of the State to provide for its own safety, and to do much for the well-being of man in his temporal and social relations; and as education is essential to the security of government, the supremacy of public law, and the enjoyment of public liberty, as well as to the individual interests of the members of the community, it becomes the duty of the State, or of the people in their civil capacity, to provide for it."[20] Ryerson's emphasis on schooling for men was not accidental: sexism regulated who received an education and who didn't.

Instead of assisting local, voluntary efforts at education, as the province had done with little enthusiasm in the Education Act of 1816, the central government now took control of standards and curriculum.[21] It was a model of public education tailored after Europe and the United States; its main outlines would be adopted later throughout Canada.

Many opposed centralized schooling. One key issue in the struggle against a centralized and "free" school system was the rights of families. Some opponents were religiously motivated. Bishop John Strachan cautioned that the common schools took from parents their "natural" right to "judge and direct" the education of children regarding religion. He argued that free schools would undermine parental responsibility. School promoters countered that since both parents and children enjoyed privileges provided by the state, society had a right to ask something in return: that all children, at the very least, attend school.[22]

The school promoters won. As historian R. D. Gidney points out, they vilified the education provided by parents for their children in rural and small-town communities. The facts show, however, that local communities hadn't been all that bad at it. In 1861, a survey of adults over the age of 20 in Canada West showed 90% were literate. This high degree of literacy was accomplished a full decade before universal compulsory

---

20. Prentice, 1977. p. 179.

21. Gidney, R. D., 1975. "Elementary Education in Upper Canada: A Reassessment" in (Eds.) M. Katz and P. Mattingly. *Education and Social Change: Themes from Ontario's Past.* New York University Press: New York. p. 21.

22. Prentice, 1977. p. 179.

schooling was established. It measures up well with that of today.[23]

The traditionalists resisted not so much the provision of education as the change in political control from local to central government. "... What the critics and reformers called flaws and weaknesses can, if examined from another perspective, be seen as perfectly comprehensible aspects of a pattern of schooling that fitted naturally into the larger context of family life and work." Gidney argues that the school promoters were caught up in the euphoria of industrial progress as they tore education away from its local roots to place it under more "progressive" centralist control. Educational improvement did not come as a natural maturing of the pioneer society but, as Gidney says, from a "new and compelling ideology of schooling" in tandem with the growth of industrial capitalism.

The new socializing thrust of the school system further undercut the traditional farming or artisan family. Increasingly separated from the world of work and increasingly fragmented in its human relationships, the traditional family couldn't effectively take on the full reproductive work of the society, and the new school system seemed to offer a realistic addition and, later, an alternative to it in many areas. Women were still to look after many reproductive functions in the home, but as they lost their productive capacities they also lost the status of being truly in charge of the more intimate running of their household. They experienced the growing involvement of experts in the family, as we noted earlier. During the early 20th century, specialists (teachers, medical experts and childcare specialists, charitable reformers, and religious leaders) reshaped childcare. Mothers now had to learn the proper methods from professionals.

This is not to set the preindustrial order on a pedestal. Its con-

---

23. Gidney, 1975. pp. 14–15. Illiteracy today in Canada, by contrast, may be close to 14–15% of the general adult population, accordingly to Robert DesLauriers. We must, however, be careful of how we compare these figures, as the criteria may vary widely. DesLauriers authored a study, "The Impact of Employee Illiteracy on Canadian Business", sponsored jointly by the Conference Board of Canada and the federal government's National Literacy Secretariat. See *Globe and Mail Report on Business*. October 14, 1990.

tradictions ran deep. The hierarchical social order oppressed women. It kept the poor "in their place" and disempowered common people. These grievances, given political expression by the Reformers, gave rise to the rebellions of 1837. In hindsight we can also see how the attachment of independent farmers and other small entrepreneurs to a larger capitalist order led them to concentrate on expansion and competition, rather than on building their power through collective action with their neighbours. Farm politics were aimed at reforming the capitalist marketplace in order to get farmers a fair share of profits, rather than to resist industrial capitalism. And, in the absence of a feminist movement, women's grievances and lack of political power went unchallenged.

The Patriarchal Split

The preindustrial family was structured by patriarchy. It was not just male-dominated, but the work of men and women was clearly split. What the family produced for sale belonged to the man; internal household matters belonged to the woman. The separation of public from private under male mastery set economic and political life ahead of family life. Men worked for society and women worked for men; female subordination was a part of family life that also led to its present crisis.

The family pervades all our perceptions of social reality, and is by no means secondary to the public realm. But the family was made out to be separate and secondary in the structures of patriarchy. This is why Elizabeth Wilson called it a "prison of love."[24] The "cult of domesticity" set up the home as a bulwark against the evils of industrialization and urbanization, with Woman pedestalized as the one fit guardian of home and hearth. But always in her place. As a reprieve from the harsh world, the home legitimized the public sphere. In cleaving the world into a public/instrumental and home/affective split, the new social order was cushioned from criticism of its oppressive public policy and practice.

These categories persist. Only since World War II, with a changing economy, including women's growing participation

---

24. Wilson, E. 1977. *Women and the Welfare State*. Tavistock: London.

in paid labour and the rise of an international organized women's movement, have these categories been seriously challenged. As Sheila Rowbotham points out in *Woman's Consciousness, Man's World*, "For a man, the social relations and values of commodity production predominate and home is a retreat into intimacy. For women, the public world belongs to and is owned by men. She is dependent on what the man earns but is responsible for the private sphere, the family."[25]

While industry required love and compassion at home to restore working men to their jobs, it also needed a high degree of individualism to spur the consumption of its rapidly proliferating goods. An aggressive individualism replaced an earlier cooperative ethic. This individualism pitted the family against itself. Michael Lerner describes how the ideology of individualism in North America is useful for capitalism: "The goal of life increasingly becomes to make it for your family. However, the ethics of self-interest soon begin to infect the family itself. Even within the same family, the more successful people begin to feel resentful at any potential obligation to the less successful."[26] Gradually, people began to think of the individual—separate from its family members and community—as being of primary value. We began to think of ourselves as separate islands, as though we were not woven into webs of dependence and responsibility.

Women In Contemporary Canadian Families

A closely linked set of family relationships and a reworked set of political and economic relations grew together with the rise of the capitalist state and industrialization. The family offered only small resistance to the expansions of consumerism and corporate profit. During the 1940's and 50's, the wage structure of industrial capitalism no longer provided a wage which could support a whole family. This loss of earning power combined with growing support for changing women's roles both enabled and required women to enter the work force. By the 1970s,

25. Rowbotham, S. 1973. *Woman's Consciousness, Man's World*. Penguin: London.

26. Lerner, M. 1986. *Surplus Powerlessness*. The Institute for Labour and Mental Health. Oakland: California.

fewer than half of all jobs paid enough to support a family.[27]

The work women do that takes place inside the confines of the private domain has always been an unacknowledged boon to the economy. Social scientists now estimate that domestic work, if measured and paid, would increase the Gross National Product by one third. But being beneath the serious consideration of economists, it has never been counted as a part of national production. Ivan Illich describes this exclusion of housework from the larger reality part of a "civil" war against vernacular values.[28]

Privileged women have been able to influence the effects of that civil war in a variety of ways, including chosing to enter the paid labour market. But most women now work outside the home (while continuing their household responsibilities) because they have to, not merely because they want to. In the past two decades, a second wage-earner has been needed not so much to "get ahead" as to avoid falling behind, especially in the 1970s when the income of Canadian wives "was the significant factor in preventing family income from dropping in real dollars."[29] In 1975 the National Council of Welfare found that if wives had not held paying jobs, the percentage of poor families in Canada would have been 51% higher than it was.[30] During recessions, even working women cannot keep their families' real incomes from slipping lower. Women have entered paid labour as a practical response to their economic needs. And this massive "feminization" of the labour market has been a boon to industry, which benefits enormously from this large flexible pool of low-paid workers.

Part of the practical need that drives women to work is the

---

27. "Today it is no longer an unwritten law of American capitalism that industry will attempt to maintain wages at a level that allows a single wage to support a family."—Christopher Lasch in "What's Wrong with the Right and the Left," *Utne Reader*, Jan./Feb. 1987, p. 86. Article printed originally in *Tikkun*, Vol. 1, No. 1.

28. Ilich, 1981, p. 115.

29. Pryor, Edward T. May 1984. "Canadian Husband–Wife Families: Labour Force Participation and Income Trends 1971–1981" in *The Labour Force*, Satistics Canada Cat. No. 71–001. Ottawa, Supply and Service Canada. pp. 93–109.

30. Pryor, 1984. pp. 93–109.

reality of the changing family. Women increasingly have had to cope on their own. Divorce and separation have created a growing number of single-parents. In 1981 single parent households made up 11 per cent of all Canadian families (compared with 9 per cent in 1971 and 6 per cent in 1961). "Single-parent" is usually the code for a mother-led family, a family that usually suffers from the lack of a decent wage or adequate child support payments.[31] Nearly half of all single-parent women were unemployed in 1985.[32] When single-parent mothers do work, they face a segregated and unequal labour market with a wage gap that sees them bring home about 60 cents for every dollar a man receives. Single-parent families are not inherently troubled families, but it is a reality that over 60 per cent of them live in poverty.

Women must also confront changing demography. By 1986 a woman on average could expect to live to the age of 78.3, while men on average died at 70.2. Men on average marry women two years younger than themselves. This means, today, that wives typically outlive their husbands by ten years. These facts, perhaps not much openly discussed, cause women without company pension plans to look anxiously ahead. What will become of them for that one eighth of life to be spent old and alone? Women's low earning power and their erratic labour force participation (since it is usually a woman's working life which accomodates the long years when children need care) mean most older women will spend several decades below the poverty line.

Besides that, child rearing takes up far less of one's time on earth than it has in the past. Part of the reason is the drop in fertility, which has been dramatic in the past 40 years with contraception.[33] That, plus longevity, has offered women a still longer span of time out from under the traditional burden of

---

31. The NDP government in Ontario has announced a new initiative for mandatory collection and enforcement of child support payments. This measure is a public acknowledgment of the disgraceful neglect by fathers of their responsibility towards children.

32. Cooke, Katie, et al., *Report of the Task Force on Child Care*. Ottawa: Minister of Supply and Services, 1986. pp. 12–13.

33. Cooke, et al., 1986, p. 5.

raising children. Back in 1850 women could expect to be with children all their married lives. By 1900 they could expect about 12 years of married life after the children left home. During the 1960s that "child-less" time grew to 23 years; today it is nearer 35.

One reason for the cutback in the fertility may well be the escalation of costs in combination with the toll on personal life. Distraught by the lack of subsidized day-care, one mother at Deux-Montagnes, Quebec, told the Katie Cooke Task Force on Child Care, "I now teach my children that they should not have kids when they marry unless they are rich."[34] One estimate puts the sheer monetary expense of taking a child from birth to the age of 21 in large metropolitan areas at about $225,000, a third of that being for daycare.[35] But aside from that, as Susan A. MacDaniel points out, women may be resisting the high cost of privatized reproduction. "Canadian women, in postponing childbearing, foregoing it altogether, or having smaller numbers of children, may be voting with their wombs that they think the price society asks of them for having children is simply too high to pay."[36]

One woman living in Toronto, Rowena Kolbathar, expressed the anguish that derives from this set of facts in a submission to the Katie Cooke Task Force. "I have a solid marriage, a good wage-earning husband and only two children," she said. "In my circumstances, you'd think the family pattern of mother as homemaker full-time would have seen its ideal fulfillment in us, yet I regard it as many years of self-sacrifice and forced imprisonment for me because there were no good alternatives and my deep sense of care and commitment to my children prohibited me from compromising and taking risks with their health and happiness. What about the miser-

---

34. Cooke, et al., 1986, p. 216.

35. Eichler, 1988, *Families in Canada Today*. 2nd Ed. Gage: Toronto. p. 330–332. *The Report of the Task Force on Child Care* by Katie Cooke et al has other figures, based on the 1984 dollar: $106,000 to raise a child from birth to age 18, including ten years of daycare.

36. MacDaniel, Susan A. 1988. "The Changing Canadian Family" in *Changing Patterns: Women in Canada*, edited by Sandra Burt, Lorraine Code and Lindsay Dorney. McClelland & Stewart: Toronto. p. 108.

ably high divorce statistics we have now? What if my husband (as many do) should decide to get rid of me and marry a younger woman? Where would I be economically without him? I have taken this risk for the sake of meeting the needs of my children, but I know it's unfair! Society has demanded much personal sacrifice from me so that I could raise my children, and if I end my days in poverty, I know that is what society has demanded of women and where we are expected to be—at the economic bottom."[37] Her letter concluded with an appeal for universally accessible childcare.

Family Issues

It would be a mistake to hold the isolated nuclear family solely responsible for its failures. The family has been abused as well as abusive. Michael Lerner notes that even as childhood is shaped by families, "our families are in turn directly and continually being shaped by the impact of work, the competitive economy, the operations of sexism and sexist ideology, and, of course, the dominant culture."[38] Yet, at the same time, the wrongs perpetrated on its members, chiefly by men on women and by both parents on children, can in no way be excused or dismissed. The problems go deep into gender relations, into the exploitative economy, and into the partitioning of human life into public and private.

Under feminist pressure to open the family to public discussion, bitter secrets began spilling out. Only in the 1970s and 80s did the full infamy of family incest and battering come to public knowledge. It delivered up sad statistics: it is estimated on good evidence that every year one in every ten Canadian women is beaten by her male partner.[39] A major study of sexual abuse of children found that one in two females and one in three males had been victims of sexual acts, and four of five of these unwanted sexual acts were first committed against these

---

37. Cooke, et al, 1986, p. 213.

38. Lerner, 1986. p. 143.

39. Roy, Marcel, et al., Standing Committee on Health, Welfare & Social Affairs, *Report on Violence in the Family: Wife Battering*. Third Report, (Hull, Quebec: Canadian Government Publishing Centre, Supply and Services Canada, May 6, 1982) p. 7.

persons as children or youths.[40] Researchers confirm that most sexual violence to children occurs at home. Sociologist Margrit Eichler estimates that at least 50 to 60 per cent of Canadian families experience some form of familial violence. Incest and battering are almost endemic to families, and the victims are mainly young children and women. That is to say, men have been the main perpetrators of the violence in this institution under their control.[41]

The acclaimed Canadian Badgley Report, a national survey, discovered that 54% of women have experienced an unwanted sexual act (one in five have survived more than one), compared to less than a third of men.[42] Diana Russell's pioneering work indicates that 19% of women will be sexually abused by a family member at some point in their life.[43] When incest occurs, 92-95% of the victims are female, and 97-99% of the offenders are male.[44] Of child sexual abuse, over half of cases occur in the home of either the victim or the perpetrator.[45]

Undoubtedly, many families do provide emotional sustenance, protection, intimacy, closeness and love. "However," sociologist Eichler says in her review of the facts, "unfortunately, there is also no doubt that much too often, far from being a haven of security and love, they constitute a brutal, exploitative environment in which the worst forms of physical and emotional intimidation and abuse take place."[46]

Accepting these facts about families, we have to use this

---

40. Badgley, Robin F., et al., Committee on Sexual Offences Against Children and Youths, *Sexual Offences Against Children in Canada*. (Ottawa: Canadian Government Publishing Centre, Supply and Services Canada, 1984) pp. 1–2.

41. A form of such violence was revealed when the New Democratic government of Ontario, newly come to power, investigated the rate of delinquent spousal support in the province. Fully 75 per cent of the 81,000 court support orders were found to be in default, for a total of $334-million in unmet payments, affecting about 80,000 children. See Linda Hossie, "Ontario cracks down on support defaulter," *Globe and Mail*, December 6, 1990.

42. Cited in Drakich and Guberman, p. 210.

43. Cited in Drakich and Guberman, p. 213.

44. Cited in Drakich and Guberman, p. 213.

45. Cited in Drakich and Guberman, p. 211.

46. Eichler, M. 1988. p. 13.

grim information to build families with stronger ties to communities that work together to support their members. If families were helped—in practical ways, through supportive public programmes and policies—they would be able to meet more of our real needs for love and connection. And if the family weren't the exclusive site of care and intimacy, more of us would be able to find places and people where support could flourish. In fact, only when people have real and viable options will we be able to fully and freely choose our families. A more caring society is part of strengthening caring families—not a way to "invade" or "destroy" families, as right-wingers claim.

In this commitment to renewed families, we reject the honouring of traditional families for crass political gains, as some governments have been inclined to do in their legislative acts and National Family Week speeches. When Alberta's Tory premier, Donald Getty, attacks the provision of public childcare as an assault on the family, we might ask how his government's commitment to free enterprise—to the point of promoting childcare for profit—supports families and children. It seems wrong to champion "family values" while supporting economic policies that destroy the communities that could help families flourish. And feminists know that "supporting the family" is often a conservative political code for service cutbacks, forcing women to do the labour that public programmes used to undertake. That kind of Tory "support for the family" is a rank sexist hypocrisy.

What remains good and important about families—their ability to offer intimacy, love and respect and to resist, in some measure, the blandishments of a commoditized public realm—needs to be recognized, respected and supported. Families have taken a beating at the hands of industrial progress; today they suffer the constant bombardment of commercial enticements, the condescending advice of social and medical authorities and the profit-oriented dictates of corporate management.

Good families—and they come in a number of forms—have important social tasks for children. Family members are "being" together rather than producing together, but they also form social purposes together. These family purposes grow into community purposes. The family can provide the foundation for what Erik Erikson called a "meaningful wider belongingness"—the extension into the world of a family's sense of what is valuable and worth fighting for. The kindness, mutuality and love that's been tested in family relations can provide a model for what ought to happen in the outside community and broader society. The differing strengths among family members, if used to the mutual well-being of all (without competition or rank) and to the resolution of conflicting desires, can provide a powerful nucleus for a child's world view.

Yet for families to do this today they need to be part of a common resistance to the isolation and fragmentation imposed on them in a capitalist social system. They can't go it alone. Public provision of childcare could help to provide practical, collective answers to the family's radical isolation.

Good families, in their many diverse forms, attempt to bring love and power together at both an intimate and a general level. The logic of such a family stands in direct opposition to the dominant social relations in a capitalist society. Such a family could be a child's first and most profound experience of group solidarity; it could be a source of a vision of a classless society. And this experience of love and the family's gift economy is as necessary for adults as for children, in our struggle to build the world we want to live in.

There is an important role for love in politics. Ontario premier Bob Rae once expressed an awareness of this by describing love and solidarity not just as "private things left to private moments."[47] Love and solidarity are public things; they can help to break the constraints of class, gender, race, upbringing and language. The love we have for one another could be expressed in social institutions and laws. And even though, for many, home has become only a nostalgic idea, Rae notes that "people everywhere persist in trying to build one up again,

---

47. Rae, Bob, "What We Owe Each Other," *Our Schools/Our Selves*, September 1990, p. 14. He wrote this as leader of the New Democratic Party before being elected premier. In a note to the NDP caucus two-and-a-half years earlier, Rae wrote: "By 1990, we need to be in a position to say 'the Liberals have failed as a party of reform. They've governed as technocrats, as bureaucrats and tinkerers, not as a party committed to working families. We've served our apprenticeship long enough. We're ready to do the job. We're ready to govern.'" See memo, "Some ideas about where we go from here," March 1988, p. 9.

attempting to preserve their identities, their individualities, unwilling to be an unknown part of a faceless mass."

Love is no mere sentiment. Love demands intelligence and insight. It often articulates itself in and around the sense of home. This may include very physical things: the walls of the dwelling, the provision of heat in winter, good food and ample clothing. But it also reaches outside the home into the material and human environment. To cut love off at the front door, by way of the age-old split of public from private, pushes back on family members those natural extensions of generosity and care, and strips them of worth in the world by making them disparage and disown their love as politics.

The intimacy, love and generosity that we know—or that we seek—at home stands in clear contrast to the competition, to contrived scarcity, to the hoarding of wealth by the imposition of poverty, to the greed and de-humanization that rules the workaday world. It requires collective action and a new language of hope to reassert the need for love in a public world antagonistic to its values, envious of its power, and devouring of its intimacies.

The Tory-Liberal spectrum of childcare, which we will explore in the following chapters, shows little understanding of this form of common-sense and love. The Tory-Liberal spectrum extends only from "welfare" to "service," as if those two concepts were the two poles of the possible in the provision of childcare. Building a community in which children, parents and other adults can give and receive equally within community has not been a part of their public agenda. In fact, that way of describing human reality is simply not within the vocabulary of government officials and those in charge of childcare professionalism. It is too messily human and democratic.

Chapter Four

The Childcare Crisis

Who Gets Hurt?

The dimensions of the childcare crisis are abstract, until you realize their real cost. Every day, families must cope with the high personal and financial cost of underfunded and inadequate childcare. They piece together patchwork solutions, and keep their fingers crossed that their arrangements don't fall through.

An example of how the current system keeps people hanging comes from the experience of Anne Thobo-Carlsen, 29, mother of a four-year-old son. She was lucky he had a place in a daycare centre near Toronto's garment district where she worked. Every morning at 7:30 Anne and her son left their Warden Woods apartment for the hour-long transit ride; she dropped him at the centre and was at her small designer contracting company by nine. The two would arrive home every night at about 7:30, twelve hours after leaving.

Anne qualified for a daycare subsidy. As a result, her son's fees were $44 a month rather than the full $525. That's how she and her husband, a warehouse shipper, still paying off school and immigration debts, made ends meet on their joint income of $1,800 a month, while sharing an apartment with her husband's brother and sister, recent immigrants from Vietnam.

When her son was four, Anne became pregnant a second

time in the confidence that another subsidized space would be available for her new child. She had no reason to think it wouldn't, but the alternative was terrifying since the full cost of infant care without subsidy would be $646 a month, enough to force her to stay home and close down her small designer contracting company. The way the system works, it is nearly always the mother who has to make that sort of sacrifice.

Anne put her name on the waiting list for subsidized daycare, but several months before the birth of her second child Metro Toronto froze all new subsidy spaces for lack of provincial funding. The freeze affected thousands of families: the waiting list in Metro Toronto contained about 4,500 names at that time. By the summer of 1991, it grew to nearly 9,000.

The last time we talked with her—when she was eight months pregnant—she did not know what would happen. Losing the space and subsidy would cost her a job and mean a drastic change in her life. Yet, as she admitted, for the present she was one of the lucky ones: her first-born had a subsidy at a centre near her place of work.

Most of the not-so-lucky families are poor. And there are a great many of them.

Statistics Canada has estimated that the average family spends 38.5% of its gross income on food, clothing and shelter. Any family that spends 58.8% of its income (twenty percentage points above the average) is defined as low-income, or below the poverty line.[1] By what the National Council on Welfare calls "conservative estimates", one in seven Canadians (3,535,000) lived on low incomes in 1987.[2] These families included 955,000 children, or nearly one in six Canadian youngsters.[3] And these were good times, before the recession struck in 1990-91. This figure, it is faint comfort to report, was down from the 1984 level of 1,209,000.[4] But by 1990, the fig-

---

1. National Council of Welfare. April, 1989. *1989 Poverty Lines*. Ministry of Supply and Services Canada. pp. 1-3.

2. National Council of Welfare. April, 1989. p. 6.

3. National Council of Welfare. April, 1989. p. 6.

4. Jack, Carolyn. September, 1990. "Children in Poverty: A Startling Profile". *Canadian Forum*. p. 17. Jack also uses figures from the National Coucil of Welfare.

ure was back up to 1,047,000.[5] Sociologist Margrit Eichler calls the stunning rate of child poverty "truly obscene, considering the fact that Canada ranks among the countries with the highest per capita income in the world."[6]

The cruelty of poverty is made even starker when we consider wealth. Almost half a million households in Canada (425,000 in 1987) reported wealth in excess of $1 million. These rich families benefit enormously from the tax system. As Marion Dewar, the Executive Director of the Canadian Council on Children and Youth, pointed out, "Recent changes to the tax system mean that taxes paid by a working poor family have increased from $175 in 1984 to $765 in 1988. By 1991, the taxes paid by that family will have increased by 369.7%, while those paid by an upper-income family will have decreased by 6.4%."[7]

The forecast on income disparity is menacing. The combined impact of the worst recession since the 1930s and the flight of jobs to the USA through Free Trade means that the picture will only grow more bleak. If Canadian job losses are any indication of the economic future of this country, growing numbers of Canadians can expect to experience the violence, anguish and humiliation that comes with poverty.[8]

Nearly half of Canada's poor families (including their children) regularly use foodbanks. Of the 378,000 people who depended on food banks every month, 151,000 (or 40%) of that number were less than 18 years old, even though children make up only a quarter of Canada's population.[9] By 1991, that figure was nearly 190,000.[10] The *Globe and Mail* says that

5. Fine, S. De 19, 1990, "One Million Children in Poverty." *Globe and Mail.*

6. Eichler, M. 1988. *Families in Canada Today.* (2nd ed.) Gage: Toronto. p. 404.

7. *Globe and Mail.* January 20, 1990.

8. Economists with the Canadian Labour Congress reported nearly two years after the free-trade pact was signed that at least 226,000 Canadian jobs had been lost as a result. See Virginia Galt, "226,000 jobs lost since pact, CLC reports," *Globe and Mail*, December 15, 1990, p. 1.

9. Michelin, L. November 20, 1989. "Children a 'shocking' proportion of Canada's hungry, survey finds," *Globe and Mail.*

10. Turner, J. September 26, 1991. "Noble words, no bold plans" *Toronto Star.* p. B.1.

children make up a "shocking proportion of Canada's hungry." The rates at which poor Canadians turn to foodbanks are climbing by 20 to 30% annually. A study by the United States Urban Institute, released recently, found that Canada has the second worst record in the industrialized world—second only to the United States—for acute child poverty.[11] Canada as a whole experienced a 25% rise in the family poverty rate from 1981 to 1984.[12] And if our governments don't understand we have a very serious problem here, the public clearly does. A poll conducted by the Globe and Mail and CBC News in October 1991, found that a substantial majority of adults—76%—supported the view that families have harder times coping these days than they used to. Asked whether families are happier than they used to be, eight out of ten respondents disagreed.[13]

When poor parents go out looking for childcare, they are especially vulnerable to what only can be described as the daycare maze.

The Daycare Maze

It is fairly simple to figure out the basics of the Canadian daycare "system." There *isn't* one. There is a hodgepodge of private and public arrangements. Across the country, from the federal down to the municipal levels of government, there is an implicit agreement that children are their parent's private responsibility. If you want to use a daycare centre, then you must pay the fees. The richer you are, of course, the wider your choices. In this paradigm, governments are simply not responsible to pay the costs of childcare—unless you qualify as needy enough under welfare legislation. Partly as a result of this, half the children in Canada are looked after by their families, usually their mothers. Sometimes they look after themselves. About one in every five children in Canada is esti-

---

11. "Thatcher left more children in poverty," *Globe and Mail*, December 14, 1990.
12. National Council of Welfare. 1985. *Poverty Profile*, 1985. Ottawa. p. 1.
13. Mitchell, A. November 5, 1991. *Globe and Mail*. p. A6.

mated to be a "latch-key child."[14]

Children who are cared for by someone other than themselves or their families are considered part of the childcare "system."[15] This system is made up of two kinds of care: "licensed" and "unlicensed." Licensed refers to daycare which meets certain provincial standards. There is a licensed childcare space for about 1 in 10 children who needs non-parental care. Unlicensed care is used by nearly 9 out of 10 children who require non-parental care. Unlicensed care is often babysitting or care by a relative or neighbour. The full responsibility for monitoring this form of care falls on parents who use the service, since there are no standards or regulations except minimal limits on size. At its best, unlicensed care can be very good; at its worst, terrible.

Even though only about 1 in 10 children needing alternate care uses licensed childcare, it is the kind of care that gathers the most attention. Since 1987, every province and territory has had some form of legislation governing childcare. Different provinces license different kinds of childcare. Daycare centres are the most common form of licensed care, but there are also other forms of care. Most provinces license daycare centres, private home daycare, and nursery schools. Some provinces also license other forms of care, like specialized preschool and school-age programmes or drop-in centres.

Licensed group centres and licensed private homes must meet provincial regulations. The various pieces of provincial legislation tend to cover a similar range of standards designed to ensure minimum quality. The most common regulations cover maximum group and centre size, child to staff ratios, minimum building specifications, staff training, and health and safety standards. Some provinces have gone further and legislated other aspects of programming, including parent involvement and cultural sensitivity. In every province and territory

---

14. Cooke, K. et al. 1986. *Report of the Task Force on Childcare.* Status of Woman Canada: Ottawa. p. 47.

15. Information on licensed childcare is drawn from the "1990 Child Care Information Sheets" published by the Childcare Resource and Research Unit at the Centre for Urban and Community Studies at the University of Toronto. They are available for sale. Contact the CRRU at 455 Spadina Avenue, Toronto, Ont. M5S 2G8.

except the Northwest Territories, having a license is a precondition before a programme may qualify for subsidies, or salary enhancement, operating or maintenance grants.

Provinces and territories enforce the licensing requirements, but the frequency of inspections and penalties varies widely among provinces. In some provinces, programmes have scheduled inspections; in other provinces, inspectors make unannounced checks. Inspectors have a great deal of discretion when it comes to acting on non-complying programmes. There is a mechanism for overseeing unlicensed programmes which come to official attention. Provincial and territorial licensing acts do have a way of regulating unlicensed care. If a programme exceeds a certain size, then it must acquire a license. Penalties for failure to comply range from reprimands or fines to being shut down by provincial authorities.

This legislative quality control system is effectively predicated on a punishment model. Failure to meet minimum standards garners fines or license revocation. A childcare programme which exceeds minimum standards by providing very high quality care—which is significantly more costly—wins no special treatment. From a business perspective, there is no systemic incentive to meet anything more than minimal standards. To treat childcare in a businesslike way practically guarantees that the deeper considerations of quality—dealing with those elusive, subjective, personal experiences of children, parents and staff—must be secondary considerations. In a commercial mentality, quality control is about ensuring that no programmes are overtly damaging or dangerous. In Chapter 6, we will consider a broader and more holisitic notion of quality.

Centres and Private Home Daycare

The two most common forms of licensed childcare are daycare centres and private home daycare. Each province and territory has legislated slightly different criteria for these two forms of care, but there are some commonalities across the country. Childcare centres provide group care, and every group childcare programme must be licensed once it passes a minimum size. A childcare centre is rarely smaller than five spaces. In British Columbia, the Yukon, and Ontario there is no maximum number of spaces. In other provinces, the maximum centre size ranges from 30 in the Northwest Territories to 80 in Alberta, with four provinces using 60 spaces as the maximum (Saskatchewan, Quebec, Nova Scotia[16] and New Brunswick.) Most provinces stipulate that daycare centres may offer full or part-day programmes, with no province permitting care for over 24 consecutive hours. Group childcare must meet the most stringent regulations of all forms of licensed care.

Private home daycare is more variable than licensed group care. Most home-based daycare isn't licensed: it is care provided informally, without public regulation. Different provinces legislated private home daycare differently. A private home may run without a license if it is small enough—although a caregiver could choose to be licensed, even for only one child. But once it is over a minimum size, then it *must* become licensed. Private home daycare is usually a one-woman operation, often a stay-at-home mother who supplements the care of her own children by taking in others. Sometimes licensed private home daycare is organized by an agency. In those cases, the agency hires the caregiver and the parents contract with the agency. Agency-based private home daycare programmes tend to have access to more resources, like staff training, toy lending, and general support.

The maximum number of children permitted in a licensed private home varies by age of child. The formula works to ensure that no single caregiver takes care of high numbers of labour-intensive infants. British Columbia, for example, stipulates that a licensed family daycare home can care for up to seven children under 12 years of age, including a maximum of five preschoolers, a maximum of two children under age 2, and one child under age 1. Every province and territory has a maximum size for private home daycare except Nova Scotia, which has no legislation to cover this kind of care. The maximum number of spaces in a licensed private home daycare ranges from a high of 8 in Saskatchewan, the Yukon, and Manitoba to a low of 4 in Newfoundland and Labrador.

Children are eligible for licensed care at different ages in

---

16. Technically, Nova Scotia only "recommends" 60 spaces as the maximum.

different provinces. Most provinces are agreed that the upper age for licensed care is 12 years. The lower end of the age range is the most variable. In Ontario, for example, children are eligible for both group and private home daycare from birth; whereas in Saskatchewan, a child cannot attend group care until 18 months. These age-eligibility criteria relate to the conflicting opinions and research on child development. The more conservative psychological literature on child development argues that "maternal separation" (never paternal!) has negative effects on infants: an expert judgment which is reflected in the restrictive legislation of some provinces.

Childcare programmes are run under different auspices. They can be non-profit, profit-making or directly operated by a branch of government. Sometimes a community group starts up a non-profit centre: sometimes there is a community board of directors, sometimes there isn't. In some provinces, the municipality will directly operate a programme as a division of its school board, community services or welfare department. A business or industry may operate a work-place childcare programme: either as a non-profit, separate division or as a part of its general profit-making operations. Large non-profit corporations can operate childcare, either as profit-making or non-profit divisions. In Canada in 1984, 14% of licensed childcare was publicly-operated, 48% was non-profit and 38% was for-profit.[17] The differences in auspices are very dramatic between provinces. For example, only 12% of Manitoba's childcare is commercial, in contrast to Alberta, where 75% of the care is profit-making. There is a raging controversy about profit-making childcare, which we will examine in more detail later in this chapter.

Who pays for childcare? The first answer is that parents do. Parents must cover the costs (if any) of unlicensed care, and they certainly must cover the cost of their fees in licensed

---

17. These figures are drawn from the Cooke report. There is no consensus on the distribution of profit-nonprofit spaces, due to controversy about accounting. "Gray areas" include programmes which are technically "non-profit", but without representative boards, or which are profit-making divisions within a larger, technically non-profit corporation. Many childcare advocates peg the *effective* percentage of for-profit care at about 50%.

childcare. However, according to Canada's major piece of welfare legislation, the *Canada Assistance Plan*, certain people may qualify for a daycare subsidy at a licensed service. The most common way that parents "prove" they deserve a childcare subsidy is by passing an income test; Ontario is an exception by employing a needs test. If a parent qualifies under an income or a needs test, some or all of their daycare fees will be subsidized through a complicated cost-sharing agreement between the federal and provincial governments, sometimes with a municipal contribution.

Even though governments will subsidize certain childcare fees, this is no recognition that childcare is a social entitlement. The basic premise of the childcare system is that it is a user-pay service. Governments may step in to take over the fees in certain cases, but this does nothing to change the basic model. This means that childcare services themselves are not funded (except in those rare, directly-operated programmes), but parents are aided at the moment of purchase. This is a hybrid, schizophrenic notion of childcare: a private purchasing decision for the most part, but one to which, under the right circumstances, governments may contribute.

Universal systemic funding would acknowledge two important facts: first, that certain services are social entitlements; second, that economies of scale must be taken into account. Neither of these sensible and practical measures characterize childcare funding.

Only Ontario and the Northwest Territories will subsidize the full amount of childcare fees; elsewhere in Canada there is a maximum limit on subsidies. And, since the tests are stringent, only the very neediest families can qualify. This means that even poor families, who have proven that they are poor enough, must in most provinces still pay a portion of their childcare fees. Moreover, simply qualifying for a subsidy doesn't guarantee that you will get one. In most provinces and in both territories, governments annually limit the number of spaces that will be subsidized within their boundaries each year, as Anne Thobo-Carlsen found out.

The National Task Force on Childcare discovered that "waiting periods of a year or more are commonplace for a subsidized space."[18] A 1987 study found that 43% of the preschool children of working parents were poor enough to qualify for a subsidy under the rules, but that only 7% of Canadian children actually got the subsidy. That's fewer than one in six.[19] In 1983, there were approximately 363,000 children under the age of 6 in families which met the eligibility criteria, and there were approximately 70,000 subsidized spots available.[20] This meant that there was a subsidy for less than one in five children who qualified—and that's not even considering the needs of eligible children aged 6 to 12 years. Governments cannot meet even their current limited financial responsibilities to qualifying parents. It will require a massive infusion of funds and a reorganization of service, before all parents have equal access to childcare services.

Parent fees are the basic source of revenue for any childcare programme which is not directly operated. The cost of daycare varies considerably. Infant care is the most expensive, since infants require the most labour-intensive care. In Ontario, the average full cost of infant care was $599/month in 1988, and has risen sharply since then. School-age children are less labour-intensive than infants (fewer staff are required), and so school-age care tends to be the least expensive. In Ontario, school-age fees in 1988 averaged $348/month. Along with child-staff ratios, the cost of childcare varies according to other expenses. The cost (and quality) of childcare obviously goes down if staff are paid poorly, if centres are under-equipped, or if children are densely packed into rooms. Most provincial licensing standards set floors to prevent this kind of poor quality care. But since almost half of the licensed childcare in Canada is operated under commercial auspices, there is a tendency to set and meet only minimum standards to ensure that the programme is lucrative. And governments seem to find it hard to insist that even these standards are seriously applied.

Overall, the daycare maze is characterized by insufficient

---

18. Cooke, et al. p. 186.

19. *Provincial Day Care Subsidy Systems in Canada*, a background document produced for the Special Committee on Child Care, chaired by Shirley Martin (Ottawa: Queen's Printer, 1987) p. 128.

20. Cooke, et al. p. 186.

numbers of expensive services. The subsidy system, which helps only a small number of the parents who need it, is stretched and under-funded. These are the objective facts which the data records. But the human impact of the childcare crisis only emerges when you talk to parents trying to find their way through the daycare maze.

One mother, Gloria Nafziger, described her search through the west end of Toronto for a place for her newborn daughter. "I started looking when I was six months pregnant," she said. Her daughter was now 17 weeks old. "My preference would have been a non-profit daycare centre. I went through the community services directory—the 'Blue Book'—and looked for a non-profit centre in our part of the city.... There weren't any.... I then contacted one or two of the commercial centres and visited one while I was pregnant: Tender Loving Care, located on Parkside. We were relatively impressed."

She put her name on the waiting list; queuing in Toronto—as all across Canada—begins before birth. In March, 1989, when we talked, Gloria's 17-week maternity leave was almost over, and Tender Loving Care had no sign of an opening.

Gloria started looking again shortly after her daughter's birth—this time for part-time care. She had decided to drop her hours at her job as a social worker with refugees at the Woodgreen Red Door Family Shelter. But this made her search even harder; no daycare centres she could find offered any part-time care. So she investigated licensed private home daycare. Gloria found several commercial private home daycare agencies with exotic names that placed children in private homes: Twinklestars, Dovercourt International, Playdough Swallows.

The people at Twinklestars had a provider. But what Gloria saw when she visited was a living room hastily rigged up for childcare, with nothing to interest a child, and the caregiver saying she was reluctant to use a stroller provided by the agency to take the children out for walks. Gloria was "not very impressed." The woman herself settled the matter by calling Gloria later to say she wasn't interested in having another child only part time.

"This was essentially the story I got from the other agencies," Gloria said. "It's hard to find a mother through an agency that wants a part-time child, because if they take a part-time child they lose one of their full-time spaces." And that, of course, means less money.

"So my third option was to go to the neighbourhood centre, the Connect Information Post. They have a childcare registry. They made no promises. They don't check anybody out. It's up to the mother to determine whether or not the home she finds is suitable." So Gloria was forced to resort to informal unlicensed care, just as 9 out of 10 Canadian families needing daycare do. Gloria got the names of 10 women willing to take a child part-time, and began calling. She interviewed five of them in person. She got lucky with the fifth.

"I found one who I think is just tremendous. I feel very, very fortunate.... I started interviewing at 12 weeks, and I was telling them that when she was 17 weeks I needed to go back to work."

The person she found had two rooms set up exclusively for children, she was willing to provide overnight and weekend care on occasion, and she gave special rates to single women. "She was going to be charging me $3 an hour.... And she's willing to be flexible.... The baby's sick, you don't pay. You go on holidays, you don't pay. That was quite exceptional to anything else I found. She also had a contract to sign." Gloria liked her businesslike approach, and the woman lived just a 10-minute drive from her house.

That's how Gloria Nafziger, social worker, found an unlicensed babysitting arrangement for her daughter in the confusing maze of childcare "options" now available. Imagine how difficult it is for someone who doesn't have Gloria's contacts.

The Debate About Commercial Childcare

The centres that exist in Canada have a variety of financial bases, but the three main categories are profit, non-profit and directly operated. The proportion of each kind varies from province to province. Overall, about 40% of Canada's licensed childcare are commercial spaces, and 60% are non-profit. About one fifth of the non-profit centres are under government auspices—municipal or provincial.[21]

These three forms of auspices differ on the relationship of income to expenses. In a non-profit programme, budgetting is designed to ensure income and expenses are equal. A directly operated programme also budgets in order to make its income equivalent to its expenses.[22] In a commercial operation, however, the childcare owner is trying to run a business. He or she aims to make a profit by ensuring that expenses are less than income—with the difference being pocketed as profit. In the unlikely event that a non-profit centre ran a surplus, it would be required by law to put those proceeds back into the centre, in the form of increasing staff wages or improving quality. Since childcare—like all human services—is labour intensive, the real margin for profit is found in cutting back on labour costs, either through low wages or high child-to-staff ratios.

Commercial, profit-making centres range from simple "mom-and-pop" operations to large childcare franchise chains. Some childcare chains are big businesses. One example of a chain is Mini-Skool, run by Kinder-Care Learning Centres, Inc. It is primarily an American operation, with 1,200 centres throughout the United States run from its headquarters in Montgomery, Alabama. Mini-Skools also has four centres in Manitoba and eight in Ontario. The Willowdale Mini-Skool franchise in Ontario has 160 children and made a profit of $60,000 in 1988. Like all licensed centres in Ontario, the Willowdale Mini-Skool was eligible for a salary enhancement grant. In 1988 the salary grant equalled about half of its profits. The Willowdale Mini-Skool paid its top qualified workers

---

21. Martin, S. et al. 1987, *Sharing the Responsibility*. Report of the Special Committee on Childcare. Ottawa: Queen's Printer. p. 35. Many school boards in Canada have made school buildings available at nominal cost for this kind of use; in Toronto alone there are 90 day-care units in public schools, most of them for school-age children. Quebec has a broad program for school-age children under auspices of the Ministry of Education. Most of the directly operated childcare is in Quebec and Ontario, with a small amount in Alberta.

22. Technically, a directly-operated programme (like a municipally-operated daycare centre) could be operated on a for-profit basis. In practice, however, this almost never occurs.

$22,500 and charged parents $6,578 a year per pre-school child in 1989.

Non-profit centres are most often run by parent/staff cooperatives, community groups, settlement houses, church groups, or municipal governments. Some operate at parents' work sites, and these are usually financed by parents with nominal assistance—often in the form of building space—from the employer. Another example of a parent community cooperative, this time in a school setting, is the Oakwood Children's House, which uses classroom space provided free of cost by a local public school in Toronto for its 24 children. All parents are part of the corporation that runs the school; they meet four times a year. The parents hire staff, set the budget—including staff salaries and parental fees—and decide on the program, which in this case is based on the ideas of Maria Montessori. This centre paid its top qualified workers about $23,000 a year, and it charged parents $5,520 a year per child in 1989.

A huge debate rages about the quality of commercial care. These questions about the quality of commercial care have significant policy implications: should scarce public dollars be allocated to free-enterprise, profit-making operators? The commercial daycare lobby argues that they provide a service exactly equivalent to a non-profit programme, and therefore they deserve equivalent treatment and access to grants. Childcare advocates and most childcare researchers rebutt this position with two different arguments. First of all, they attack the claim that the service is equivalent by pointing out that the quality of care in commercial operations is nearly always inferior to non-profit or directly operated care.[23] Secondly, they argue against private profits being made from childcare

---

23. Laurel Rothman, as president of the Ontario Coalition for Better Child Care, laid the research on this before the Special Parliamentary Committee on Childcare in 1988. In one study, inspectors were asked to rate 1,000 centres on such things as child development, nutrition, service to parents, safety and working conditions. They rated non-profit higher than commercial care in virtually all measures they used. Another researcher studied 431 licensed centres in Metro Toronto, both non-profit and commercial, and found the non-profit staff better trained and the centres better run. The research found 54% of the commercial centres with too few staff (below the provincial standard), compared to 15% of the non-profit centres.

and public money.[24]

Most of the profit/non-profit debate is framed within the "objective" and neutral criteria of good childcare. Commercial childcare is largely fought with the language of social policy. Martha Friendly, a Canadian childcare researcher, states that "for-profit status is a main predictor of poorer quality."[25] She means that commercial care scores lower than non-profit care when measured against objective criteria of turn-over rates, staff salaries and benefits, working conditions, staff training, staff/child ratios, group size, health status, and observed measures of quality programming. The childcare movement also pinpoints the low wages of childcare workers who in the mid-1980's earned, nation-wide, $13,000/year in non-profit centres compared to $11,000/year in commercial centres.[26] Using this empirical data, the childcare movement argues that the quality of commercial care is too low.

Another argument widely used against commercial care is that spending public funds to support private profits is "inefficient." Action Day Care pints out that "As long as public money in the form of purchased daycare subsidies is available to these programmes, they are tax-supported without public accountability."[27] The Canadian Daycare Advocacy Association says that commercial care is "a poor use of public dollars,

---

24. In another place, Susan Prentice points out that another basic contradiction in government aid to commercial daycare is that it nourishes with public money a lobby of commercial operators that have worked "to downgrade government standards and regulations to increase their profitability." The free enterprise lobby, she points out, "has been effective in keeping a regressive pressure on standards in the United States, and was pivotal in a key daycare struggle in Ontario in 1974 over the 'Birch poposals.'" See "The 'Mainstreaming' of Daycare," *Resources for Feminist Research*, September 1988, p. 60.

25. Friendly, M. 1986. "Daycare For Profit: Where Does the Money Go?" Brief to the Special Parliamentary Committee on Childcare. Toronto. p. 22.

26. These were the figures the Katie Cooke Task Force discovered in 1986. Recent provincial initiatives have resulted in big jumps in worker wages in the five years since the Task Force. Wages, however, are still very low and reflect neither the importance of the job, nor the skills it requires.

27. Action Day Care. March, 1984. *Action Day Care Newsletter*. p. 7.

and poor public policy."[28] Martha Friendly argues

> In a for-profit program, the decisions about spending money are business decisions and accountability is not part of the process.... Second, there is no advantage to Canadian families in straining already scarce public revenues by allowing a portion of dollars which are intended for childcare services to find their way into the pockets of owners, especially if, as so many people have recommended, a larger proportion of childcare dollars become publicly supported.[29]

Advocates also say that the "choice argument" of the free-enterprise lobby—the idea that parents choose commercial care and that those choices must be respected—is misleading. Parents often lack adequate information with which to assess quality. Only a certain class of parents have the right to "choose". The market is a realm of free choice only for those people who have financial access to all its options. Without adequate resources to purchase care, and without service in all neighbourhoods and communities, arguements about free choice are meaningless.

With these arguments in hand, many childcare advocates believe that a frontal attack on the morality of profit-making childcare will do more harm than good. In a free-enterprise society, they argue, it is impractical to spend much effort opposing a profit-making perspective. Action Day Care put it this way: "Action Day Care and groups like it which have opposed daycare for-profit have not taken this position for purely ideological reasons. Rather, when one examines the issues of quality and use of public dollars, it is apparent that there is at least a suspicion that concerns about for-profit daycare is a practical matter."[30]

Sheila Kamerman, the foremost American childcare researcher, reports that "childcare should be defined as a 'practi-

---

28. CDCAA. 1987. *Childcare for Profit: Why We Oppose It.* A document co-sponsored by the CDCAA, NAC, and the Ontario Coalition for Better Day Care.

29. Friendly, M. May, 1986. p. 23-27.

30. Action Day Care. March, 1984. "Profit-making Daycare: What's Wrong With It?" *Action Day Care Newsletter.* p. 7.

cal' rather than a 'moral' issue and advocated as such."[31] The National Action Committee on the Status of Women (NAC) opposes commmercial care "based on the fact that the quality of care in profit centers is, in general, lower than the quality of care in non- profit centres."[32]

The "quality" and "efficiency" arguments against commercial childcare are complex and difficult to assess. On the one hand, they are correct, since a substantial body of research indicates that the "quality" and "efficiency" of commercial care is lower than non-profit care. On the other hand, the use of neutral empirical language avoids the political and ethical issues of collective childcare.

When you follow the threads, you see how support for commercial daycare leads inevitably to a free-enterprise zone in childcare, with quality for the rich and zoo-keeping for the poor. Support for non-profit childcare, in contrast, can go in two directions, and we have to choose between them. One direction leads to a top-down hierarchy dominated by experts and professionals and large institutions. The other direction leads to lively and democratic community-based participation of parents and workers.

The profit/non-profit debate goes much further than locking horns over which auspices provide higher "quality" and "efficiency." It forces us to figure out exactly what these terms mean. Margaret O'Brien Steinfels notes that parent and community control may seem a marginal point about administration. "But," she argues, "the question of parental and community involvement, is, in fact, the single most important, albeit acrimonious discussion about daycare.It asks, in effect, 'Who will raise our children?'"[33]

In a caring society, childcare could not be a commodity. It would operate by the logic of community service, not the market. This would totally reorganize how the service was delivered. Childcare which is "of the community, by the communi-

---

31. Kamerman, S. May-June, 1985. "Childcare Services: An Issue for Gender Equity and Women's Solidarity." *Child Welfare*. Vol. LXIV, no. 3. p. 265.

32. NAC. March 18, 1986. *NAC Childcare Bulletin*.

33. O'Brien Steinfels, M. 1973. *Who's Minding the Children? The History and Politics of Daycare in America*. p. 114.

ty, and for the community" would have the community taking part in setting programming, hiring staff, developing job descriptions, establishing programme philosophy, and starting services that meet its needs.

We oppose commercial childcare even if it were, in a technical sense, high quality. We want to transform the social division of labour involved in caring for our children. Universal care which is not community-based remains partial. Commodified childcare would not be satisfactory even if there was a space for every child who wanted or needed one. Similarily a non-profit childcare system that relied on staff exploitation to keep fees low would be unacceptable.

We will turn to the question of quality, as well as parent and community involvement, in Chapter 6. But it is important to state clearly that the non-profit/commercial debate offers a valuable opportunity to draw out the fundamental differences in the philosophies of care. When progressive people hide their politics behind the "scientific" evidence of quality, and stay silent on the real issues that fuel the intense debate, we miss the chance to put our case forward. How will we popularize our message about sharing the caring, if we hesitate to give full voice to our democratic vision?

The Invisible Funding Labyrinth

There are several reasons for the complication of public childcare financing in Canada. Canada is a far-flung and various country that requires complex granting formulae. The country contains divergent cultural traditions as well as varied levels of poverty and wealth. Childcare financing must accommodate all of that. Funding is also complicated by the several levels of government involved and the uneasy saw-off of powers between provincial and territorial and federal governments.

It is further complicated by the fact that it was set up for a number of different (and sometimes conflicting) reasons: to boost child-bearing by women, to keep women at home and out of the labour force, to redistribute economic wealth either upward or downward, to attempt to eliminate poverty, to enable women to join the job market, and, lately, to assuage the clamour for federal assistance to childcare. (The aim of giving children the best possible deal is usually thrown in as a worthy afterthought. The goal of women's full liberation, or a democratic distribution of social care, never even gets on the agenda.)

Mainly, of course, as we've described it, childcare is not funded publicly; it is paid for by parents. This also complicates matters. Almost all childcare in Canada that is paid for at all is offered on a fee-for-service basis. Parents who get assistance from government have to apply for that assistance themselves. With or without that assistance in hand, parents must pay whatever it costs in a non-profit centre and whatever the owner asks in a commercial centre. (Though in each case the province may provide some grants directly to centres toward staff salaries.) In Ontario, fees may range from $5,000 to $9,000 a year per child.

Subsidies are funded through a tortuously complicated scheme. Basically, childcare subsidies are part of the Canadian welfare state's cost-sharing programmes. These are welfare measures which are jointly paid for by the federal and provincial governments and authorized by the Canada Assistance Plan (CAP). The CAP was instituted in 1966 during the Lester Pearson years as an attempt to improve the lot of the poor. Childcare provisions were only part of the Liberal "war on poverty." In these provisions the federal government pays half of every eligible dollar. "Eligible" dollars are carefully defined: parents must qualify under an income or a needs test; they must use their subsidy at a licensed space; and the province must agree to match the federal contribution. Welfare funding is targetted, not universal. Unlike health care or education, to which everyone is entitled, childcare subsidies are only available to the needy.

If a provincial government won't cough up its 50% share, then parents in that province can't use the "offer" of federal subsidies.[34] Several provinces, including Ontario, have passed the cost of welfare down to municipalities. In Ontario, for example, towns and cities that offer daycare put in 20 cents and

---

34. The current Conservative government is proposing to dramatically change the Canada Assistance Plan. Because the changes are still in process, it is hard to predict the final shape. What seems clear is that the potential generosity of CAP will be cut back, the richer provinces will have their contribution "capped", and the universal portability philosophy will be eliminated.

the province pays 30 cents of every subsidy dollar. Parents who qualify for the subsidy nearly always still pay something for childcare, but only what municipal or provincial officials think they can afford. The subsidy pays the rest. But with tight provincial or federal money, the subsidies don't multiply as fast as daycare needs do. If the province or the municipality refuses or is unable to contribute, the federal dollars go unspent.

The way all this works is shown in the case of Linda and Steve Burdett, who received subsidized childcare for three-year-old Lianne at Central Neighborhood Daycare in Toronto, but after a second child came they had to plead with Metro authorities for four-and-a-half months to get the same service for 14-month-old Daniel—because daycare spaces were in such short supply. They needed daycare because Steve's salary of $15 an hour as foreman for a landscape company simply wasn't enough. Their phone had been cut off twice, and they had trouble keeping up with their rent. The daycare finally accepted Daniel and offered a subsidy that brought the total $270 weekly fee down to an affordable $15. At this point, Linda quickly got a $10-an-hour receptionist job. But as soon as she reported this, daycare authorities moved to reduce the subsidy. At the time we spoke with her, the new daycare rate had not yet been determined.

The system of subsidized daycare is piecemeal, but the main problem is that while many call on it, few are chosen. You can be ever so poor and get your name on the list for a subsidy, but if there's no centre or agency with a licensed space for your child, you won't get the subsidy nor a place for your child. The shortage of spaces in most provinces is massive and chronic. The waiting list for subsidized daycare spaces in Metro Toronto, for example, was nearly 9,000 in the spring of 1991.

A 1987 study found that 43% of the preschool children of working parents qualified for a subsidy under the federal CAP rules, but only 7% actually got the subsidy. That's fewer than one in six.[35] This is not to say that the parents of all 43%

---

35. *Provincial Day Care Subsidy Systems in Canada*, a background document produced for the Special Committee on Child Care, chaired by Shirley Martin (Ottawa: Queen's Printer, 1987) p. 128

would have applied; many parents might still opt for informal care with relatives or friends. But the figures show that for all the gradual expansion by the provinces at the funding end of things, childcare is severely restricted by the sheer lack of funds and licensed spaces.

Other Assistance

Subsidies to parents are not the only way the federal government provides funds.

First of all there's the "baby bonus," formally called the Family Allowance, which gives about $380 a year to families with children under 18. "This measure proceeds upon the assumption that children are an asset to the state," Prime Minister Mackenzie King declared when he set up the allowance as an inducement to women to have more babies. In the scheme of things these days, the baby bonus is no great boon to the individual family, though it does help. Yet it has created a bill of $2.6-billion a year from the government.[36]

A second way government funds childcare is through a system of tax deductions and credits. The tax deduction lets parents deduct from their income taxes some of the money they spend for childcare. There's a ceiling on it, but beneath that ceiling every childcare receipt they can show to the tax department will reduce taxable income by the amount spent.

Governments tinker a lot with tax schemes; here is how the Katie Cooke Task Force described recent federal footwork on tax exemptions for childcare:

> The tax exemption itself has been variously increased, replaced with a tax credit, abolished, reintroduced, indexed to the Consumer Price Index, de-indexed, and now partially indexed. The family allowance was introduced, increased, taxed, indexed, de-indexed, indexed again, reduced, index-limited to 6% in 1983 and 5% in 1984, re-indexed and finally partially de-

---

36. The Tories' 1989-90 federal budget breached the heretofore universality of this program—wherein all families received the same amount for each child—by taxing back the allowance of those families with earnings above a specified level. And the government further saved itself $300-million by deciding to index benefits not to the increase in cost of living, as previously, but to the amount of annual inflation over 3%. See Michael Valpy, "Figures shed light on Wilson's budget" *Globe and Mail*, May 2, 1989.

indexed. A child tax credit was introduced in 1977; increased, made refundable and income-tested in 1978; increased again in the 1982 and 1985 budgets, with the income test being first indexed, then frozen and finally reduced.[37]

Since the income tax is set at a higher percentage for those with higher incomes, this means—dollar for dollar—richer families get a bigger break than poorer parents do. Let's say two families each had receipts of $4,000 one year for daycare, but that one family had $45,000 in taxable income and the other family $27,500. The richer family would get back $1,040 for its daycare receipts; the poorer family would get back only $650. That makes this measure in itself "regressive"—for dollars spent, it helps well-to-do parents more than it helps the poor.[38] This scheme was bequeathed to the Tories by the Liberals, but the Tories expanded it despite the fact that the Tory-dominated Special Committee on Child Care recommended in 1987 that it be abolished.

The child tax credit is money that goes straight to parents with children under six years old, presumably so that they can purchase "informal" childcare with it. They don't have to show receipts; they get the money anyway. This goes exclusively to low- and middle-income parents.

Another source of childcare funds are the provinces themselves, depending on how generous the government of the day has decided to be. The province may make a contribution beyond its share of the CAP subsidy. These generally come in the form of a "direct operating grant," a cash payment that flows straight to the childcare programme, allowing it to increase staff salaries, reduce parent fees, or both. This varies greatly with each province, and some provinces make no grants at all.

Under Liberal and NDP governments of recent years, Ontario stepped up a series of worker salary-enhancement initiatives. The NDP tied new grants for workers' salaries in

---

37. Cooke, 1986, p. 177.
38. Blain, Christine. 1985. "Government Spending on Child Care in Canada," Series 1, *Financing Child Care: Current Arrangements, Background Paper to the Report of the Task Force on Child Care*. Ottawa: Status of Women.) p. 183 ff.

November 1991 to a commitment by commercial operators to switch to the non-profit system. This drew an outcry from the provinces' 645 commercial operators, but Marion Boyd, Minister of Community and Social Services, declared it a move toward a universal system "in which there is an entitlement to childcare."

All of this government money is hardly enough to make the childcare system adequate or universally accessible. If you divide the total 1985 governmental outlay of $542.3 million by the 507,000 children in Canada under the age of six with both parents in full-time work or study, you would get about one-fourth of what it cost to keep a three-year-old in daycare for a year. And that excludes children from six to twelve who might need part-time daycare. The Katie Cooke Task Force found that there were licensed spaces in Canada for fewer than 10% of the children under 13 requiring full-time or out-of-school care, should their parents desire licensed care for them.

Chapter Five

A Brief History of Childcare Services

Child care is not merely a contemporary response to the current economic situation. Child-care services have existed in Canada for well over one hundred and fifty years.[1] If we look at that history, we will see how various progressive moments came and went, and how the childcare movement gained its present shape and momentum.

Forces providing childcare have included the state, conservative charities, social reformers and women's groups. Rationales among them for providing childcare have ranged from a conservative emphasis on social control and prevention of poverty to a feminist understanding of the relationship of childcare to women's liberation.

Mothers have always worked, and children have always needed care. Most of this care has been and is informal. But formal childcare services have existed in Canada since 1854

---

[1] This chapter relies on Pat Schulz's 1978 article, "Daycare in Canada: 1860-1962", in Kathleen Gallagher-Ross (Ed.) *Good Daycare*. Women's Press: Toronto, one of the few histories of Canadian daycare. Pat Schulz also deposited a significant collection of historical material with the Metropolitan Toronto Reference Library which has also been used here. The chapter further draws on research conducted for Susan Prentice's Ph.D. dissertation, *Militant Mothers in Domestic Times: Toronto's Postwar Daycare Fight*. (Sociology, York University). Primary sources are not cited, although published secondary sources are noted.

when the Grey Nuns in Montreal opened a creche. The primary purpose of the Creche d'Youville was to provide care for the children of working parents as well as to provide religious education. The first English-speaking creche, the Montreal Day Nursery, opened in 1887, with the City of Toronto following shortly after in 1891 with the Toronto Creche and in 1892 with East End Creche. These early childcare centres were run as charities designed to serve working mothers. An important feature of early childcare centres was the domestic employment bureau, an auxiliary service run by the supervising agency to provide employment to mothers whose children would be cared for in the nursery. The combination of day nurseries and maternal employment provided a solution to a pressing problem of the middle-class: the "servant shortage."

Although the main purpose of these childcare centres was to provide some measure of direct relief to the working class, they were also seen as a way to prevent social problems. Early reformers argued that better childcare would help stamp out delinquency, criminals, mental diseases and the social vice of poverty.

Early centres, however, were largely damaging places for young children by contemporary standards. Childcare programming and the principles of good early childhood education were unknown. Most programmes served only one meal, yet children were often in care for up to twelve hours daily. As late as 1930, children at Toronto's Victoria Day Care Services were only receiving a vegetable soup in which a bone had been cooked, a piece of bread without butter, and a pudding or fruit. Programmes were understaffed. Toronto's West End Creche, for example, in 1909 provided 5,539 days of childcare and provided 3,160 days of employment for mothers, with a staff of only "a matron, a nurse and cook, and a housemaid." Children were subjected to strict discipline and authority, and strenous attempts were made to train them into the manners and mores of the middle class.

Women's philanthropic organizations were vital to the establishment of childcare and other social services. Women could often legitimate their social and political works in the supposedly male public realm by appeals to the notion of "social housekeeping"; the extension of women's "normal" maternal role to the world at large.[2] To circumvent male critiques of women's activism, organizations would frequently establish a "legitimate" male advisory board of experts, such as clergy and businessmen, while the daily operation of the centre was managed by an all-woman management board. For example, East End Creche was run by a "member's club" of between forty and fifty women and was governed by a twelve-man advisory board.

Policy decisions about enrollment reveals an interesting progression of thought on child development. Throughout the 20th Century, as sexist research on child development "proved" the damaging effects of maternal separation, centres increasingly refused to accept very young children. For example, West End Creche must have enrolled infants at its founding in 1909 because later documents record a 1932 decision to limit enrollment to children over one year. This was because: "It is an accepted fact among pediatricians that it is impossible to give the young infant the necessary careful handling with run-clear children in the same room." In 1950, West End Creche's Annual Report records a decision to limit enrollment to children over the age of two-and-a-half years. The rationale was that "younger children are not yet ready to leave the close personal relationship of the home and were too young to benefit greatly from the group programme." These policy decisions mirror changes in women's labour force participation rates and in the ideology of appropriate sex roles and motherhood.

Involvement by Canadian governments in the funding of childcare began around the turn of this century. West End Creche received a $500 founding grant from the City of Toronto in 1909 and annual voluntary grants from that year onward. In 1919, the Centres des Petites in Montreal reported that it received a grant of 2 cents per day per child (at a time when daily costs were 10 cents, this represented 20% of operating costs), and documents indicate that this grant had been in oper-

---

2. Gordon, L. 1982. "Why 19th century feminists didn't support 'birth control' and 20th century feminists do: Feminism, reproduction and the family." In (Ed.) Thorne, B. and M. Yalom. *Rethinking the Family*. Longman: New York.

ation for some time. The first formal state involvement in the on-going operation of a centre occurred in Vancouver. In 1910, a creche was established, jointly organized by Associated Charities and the City of Vancouver. For six years it was run under joint management; in 1916, it was passed over to the jurisdiction of the City of Vancouver Health Department.

The Contradictions Of Early Childcare

Contradictions plagued the early childcare organizers. Their class biases were unmistakeably imprinted in the services they offered. Most middle-class reformers would never have dreamt that working-class children in their centres deserved the same quality as their own middle-class children. Reformers resented it when recipients of their charity challenged the quality of the care they gave. Pat Schulz, an historian, documents instances of mothers being threatened with dismissal from their jobs and corresponding expulsion of their children from the day nursery for "insubordination" or "insolence." Minutes of the East End Creche record a debate over the eligibility for enrollment of a mother's second illegitimate child. The class gap between service providers and service users was unbridged.

By the end of the nineteenth century, day nurseries were firmly established. Their overt function was to benefit and encourage the working poor. Equally important was their role in a system of social control and regulation of the poor. Reformers of the late 19th century operated from what today would be called a kind of maternal feminism strongly flavored by classist and racist politics. Their admonitions of self-help, piety, moral virtue, and valorization of the family were widely-held views. Early childcare movement reformers grew to accept the necessity of public funding to subsidize the high cost of care, but primarily saw childcare as a service to enable families to become economically self-sufficient and to instill the values of discipline and self-control in children. Despite this perspective, 19th century reformers also understood childcare as a service to working women who were burdened by external economic factors. It was not until the early part of the 20th century, that childcare became more unambiguously stigmatized as responding to a pathological family problem.

During this latter period, the day nurseries and day nursery movement declined across North America. Parallel, however, to this decline was a rise in the Nursery School Movement, a specifically middle-class model of care. The earliest nursery school was established in 1915 at the University of Chicago by a group of faculty wives. Their mandate was: "to offer an opportunity for wholesome play for their children, to give the mothers certain hours of leisure from childcare, and to try the social venture of cooperation of mothers in childcare."[3]

"The social venture of cooperation" was a potential window into a collective vision of childcare. Yet well-educated, privileged women who wanted "leisure from childcare," contrasted sharply with working-class mothers who used day nurseries because they worked outside the home. The chasm between elite nursery schools (with stay-at-home mothers) and working-class childcare was enormous. Any progresssive potential for alliances between the Nursery School and the childcare movement did not materialize. Instead, the schism between stigmatized childcare centres for the needy and educational enrichment through part-day nursery schools for the middle-class widened.

Day nurseries continued unchanged through World War I, largely because the demand for female labour continued to make such childcare necessary. One Toronto centre pointed out in 1916 that "employment of mothers is so high that for the first time we couldn't supply the demand for women to do day work [domestic labour]." We can assume that many of these women were engaged in work related to the war, although labour participation rates by women nowhere approached the record levels of World War II.

Childcare began to be professionalized during the early part of the century through the burgeoning study of developmental psychology. A changing awareness of the educational possibilities for young children led to calls by educational reformers for staff training. In 1926, the Toronto Institute of Child Study was established to train childcare workers. As Pat Schulz documents, applicants for childcare were no longer considered poor but hard-working people who needed a particular service.

---

3. Turner, J. 1982. *Daycare and Women's Labour Force Participation: An Hisorical Study*, unpublished Master's Thesis. University of Regina. p. 51

"In the eyes of social workers they became, at best, people who were unable to decide for themselves what kind of help they needed; at worst, they were considered to be lazy or fraudulent."[4] This later movement of professionalization twinned childcare with welfare and stigmatized the service.

Changing State Policy

State childcare policy was premised on ideas of the "normal" family and the "normal" roles of mothers. In economic terms, the idea of "the family" was ensconsed in the "family wage" and the ideology of familialism. Both the family wage and the Mother's Allowance Bill of 1920 were designed to "protect" and promote families with stay-at-home mothers. Day nurseries in Ontario in the early 20th Century "represented a condensation point for the contradictions of the family wage ideology." There was an enormous contradiction between state childcare policy and the reality of most people's lives. Steve Milton says that "In all cases day nurseries navigated the contradictory waters of the family wage ideology with an eye to enforcing a particular sexual division of labour, as well as maintaining a certain standard of reproductive practice."[5]

World War II dramatically changed the situation of childcare in Canada.[6] For the first time the federal government became involved in childcare through a 1942 order-in-council which established federal-provincial childcare cost-sharing. Only Ontario and Quebec took advantage of the funds to establish childcare centres. During the war, twenty-eight day nurseries were opened in Ontario, and six in Quebec. The remaining provinces argued that they were insufficiently industrialized to need childcare. Childcare was support for the "war effort," not for working parents or women, as evidenced by the fact that in order to receive support, at least 75% of the children in care had

---

4. Schulz, p. 149.

5. Milton, S. 1986. *Ontario's Daycare Policy, Ideology, and Women's Work*. M.A. thesis, University of Toronto. p. 151.

6. An important book, which records some of the impact of the war on childcare service provision, is Ruth Pierson's, *"They're Still Women After All": The Second World War and Canadian Womanhood*. 1986. McClelland and Stewart: Toronto.

to have mothers working in "essential" (read: war) industry.
Aggressive propaganda encouraged women to enter paid employment. Women entered the labour force in massive numbers and regulated childcare blossomed. Government policy conceded that childcare was a social responsibility, but only under exceptional circumstances. Mrs. Fraudena Eaton, the government official responsible for recruiting women, acknowledged: "Consistent and well-founded reports lead one to believe that children are neglected—thus becoming unhappy, undernourished and delinquent. Such a situation must be accepted as a responsibility of government in these days, when it has become a burden too heavy for private agencies."

The end of the war in Canada was marked by state adoption of two radical new approaches: Keynesian full employment and a host of new social welfare policies. A major part of intensive post-war policies to promote economic growth was the elimination of women from the paid labour force. In its bluntest form, this was carried out through the closure of the war-time nurseries. Abruptly, the governments of both Quebec and Ontario declared that all day nurseries would be closed.

The state was not prepared to finance day nurseries or the role for women they supported, despite the documented high need. One survey conducted in September 1945 of 542 working mothers showed that 89% of them intended to work indefinitely, nearly all for economic reasons. State moves were clearly based on sexist notions of family and class-biased perceptions of why women worked. The *Globe and Mail* reported that "While the Provincial Government has expressed concern that any deserving cases should suffer from the cessation of the plan, welfare officials are agreed that whenever possible mothers shouldn't shirk their responsibility in caring for their children at home in order to boost what is already an equitable income by working daily. 'We believe that a child should be brought up in the proper enviroment in its own home, when possible' said one official."

Despite a huge public outcry in Quebec, all French centres were closed. In Ontario a well-organized Day Nursery and Day Care Parents Association in 1946 led a militant protest that saved sixteen of twenty-eight pre-school centres. All forty-two school-age programmes were closed, although eight re-opened shortly afterwards.

The Day Nursery and Day Care Parents Association, formed in Toronto, was the first contemporary example of progressive childcare organizing. The Association held the first daycare demonstration, a march to Queen's Park on May 10 1946, to protest the closures of war-time nurseries. It organized public meetings, lobbied both the Toronto Board of Education and the Separate School Board to support the campaign to prevent the closures, and hosted a public speaker series. A vigorous campaign won the support of the municipal politicians in the City of Toronto. The Association undertook a lively public relations campaign with high-profile meetings, deputations, and letters to the editor. In addition to lobbying on policy issues, the Assocation worked to improve the quality of care in centres through attention to issues of programming and staffing.

In 1946, the Province of Ontario passed the Day Nurseries Act, which established minimum regulations and standards for day nurseries. Relatively high standards, coupled with a lack of provincial funds, resulted in the closure of many centres. While regulation was supported by the Association, it argued that regulation in the absence of resources sabotages childcare. In 1950, Mrs. Isobel Bevis of the Day Nursery and Day Care Parents' Association argued that "investigations, screenings, and petty regulations are being used by City Welfare Department in a futile attempt to reduce the numbers of families using day nurseries."

The ambivalent approach of the province was never hidden. The province's day nurseries consultant, the former assistant director of the Institute for Child Study, said that childcare was a passing phenomenon, to be tolerated temporarily to help families to achieve an adequate level of "mental hygiene." Eventually, she said, "For future generations of children our aim is to increase the possibility for full home life, thus reducing, finally, the need for day care."

Janet Turner calls the two decades after the war the doldrum years of childcare organizing in Canada. Pat Schulz says that by 1962 the gains of the Second World War had almost entirely disappeared. Women with children had retreated in large numbers from the paid labour force. High childcare fees, the aggressive ideological campaigns of the 1950s, the rise of suburbanization, and economic prosperity that permitted many women to remain at home out of the paid labour force contributed to a lessening of demand for childcare. Ideological arguments about the effects of childcare on young children were buttressed by the sexist research of John Bowlby and others who determined that severe "maternal deprivation" occurred in childcare programmes, scarring children for life. This provided the decisive proof for the campaign begun much earlier to keep children at home, out of organized childcare. Throughout this period the small organized Canadian women's movement paid little attention to childcare issues, despite both high labour-force participation and rising divorce rates that left many women without resources to meet child-rearing expenses.

A Break From The Past

The childcare movement of the early 1970s marked a decisive break from previous organizing.[7] A new childcare movement arose from the organizing which flourished in the period. It gave rise to a massive expansion of childcare services. The heyday of cooperative childcare organizing led to the establishment of a number of explicitly radical childcare centres. Unlike earlier childcare philosophies, the idea that "children are only littler people" took root in major urban centres, notably Vancouver and Toronto. Informed by a rapidly rising feminist consciousness, well-versed in the New Left, these childcare centres were independent and radical care cooperatives that struggled for anti-sexist, anti-racist, and anti-authoritarian programming and process. While enormous contradictions existed between theory and practice, between radical rhetoric and behaviour (which often reproduced traditional values and attitudes), the era established a new political perspective on childcare.

With the turn of the 1980s and a changed political reality, a newly-sober childcare movement emerged. Across the country, provincial coalitions formed. A movement away from small-

---

7. See, for an example, M. Killian's "The Louis Riel Cooperative, Or Children Are Only Littler People" In *Women Unite.* 1972. Women's Press: Toronto.

scale community solutions towards a larger policy framework was completed. This is the moment when the language of a universally accessible, publicly-funded, high quality, non-profit, non-compulsory, community-based childcare system was cemented among childcare advocates.

At the same time, a change in emphasis occurred inside the practical politics of the childcare movement. The issue of "universal" care was moved into the background. The spotlight was now on the issue of profit or non-profit daycare. The emerging agenda was to identify "quality."

Public awareness about the positive benefits of, and need for, childcare began to change during the 1960s when a study found 800,000 children in Canada with both parents holding outside jobs. At that point the minority Liberal government of Lester Pearson started helping some children attend daycare through the Canada Assistance Plan. It's aim was to provide welfare services "having as their object the lessening, removal or prevention of the causes and effects of poverty, child neglect or dependence on public assistance," as the Act itself set out its aims.

This assisted the poor, but it offered little to middle-class mothers who increasingly had to take outside jobs to keep their families out of poverty. The Royal Commission on the Status of Women warned in 1970 of a coming childcare crisis, and declared that "the time is past when society can refuse to provide community childcare services in the hope of dissuading mothers from leaving their children and going to work."

Back then, 20% of all mothers with children under 14 held outside jobs. Today, fully 60% of all mothers are in the labour force. But the federal government clings to the same basic welfare system that it started 25 years ago, with the addition of nominal tax deductions and credits for childcare expenses.

Today, there are over 300,000 licensed childcare spaces in Canada. Every province and territory has legislation licensing childcare provision and standards. There are childcare advocacy organizations in every major Canadian city and in every province and territory. There is no doubt that the issue of childcare has come of political age. And yet, the crisis of affordability and access, as we have argued in previous chapters, has not been resolved.

Chapter Six

Political Responses

When it comes to promises, everyone is for childcare. During the 1984 federal election, leaders of all three political parties declared their support during a televised debate sponsored by the National Action Committee on the Status of Women. There have been two high profile research projects at the national level. Provincial governments, too, have responded with initiatives. Municipalities are responding to the needs for service in a variety of ways.

This social acknowledgement is gratifying. There is no mistaking the fact that the childcare movement has seen the state throw its support—at least at the rhetorical level—behind advocates' demands.

And yet, the childcare crisis persists. What explains this seeming contradiction?

The Canadian welfare state is a paradox. It must stand by its political legacy of liberal democracy with equality and justice for all. And yet, it must ensure that the economic system of private wealth and class disparity is not challenged. This means it must appear to support the "common good" and the national "best interest" by appearing responsive, flexible and conciliatory. At the same time it must make sure the privileged and the powerful remain undisturbed.

Somewhere in the middle of these contradictory tasks of accumulation and legitimation, the state develops policies and funding for childcare. Only those forms of childcare that contribute to the maintenance of the current social order will readily be underwritten by the state. Thus when the state appears to be dealing with women's issues, children's rights and social justice it often responds with policies that actually undermine those social movements.

With several decades of childcare organizing behind us, we can see that some "reforms" don't reform anything at all, while certain policies have actually worked against childcare advocates. When advocates lobbied for a direct grant to improve cash-starved conditions in community childcare programmes, commercial operators were duly assisted as well. When advocates demanded public dollars to raise worker wages, the profits in commercial operations rose alongside worker salaries. As advocates worked to get school boards and municipal governments to directly operate childcare programmes, community-based control was lessened. The federal government responded to parents' demands for financial assistance by implementing childcare credits that do nothing to ensure that there are more licensed spaces.

In spite of this level of government resistance, long-term childcare organizing has had many positive results. As the childcare issue becomes increasing "mainstream," childcare funding and service is also increasing. There is no doubt that there was more and better childcare in 1990 than there was in 1980, or that it was brought about by the combined efforts of governments and childcare advocates. The childcare movement has successfully convinced the government to initiate policies and programmes to increase state support for childcare. But just as we are now beginning to understand the limits of reforms like pay equity and advisory councils, so we need to be vigilant about the kind of reforms which shape or fail to reshape the emerging childcare system.

The Task Force On Childcare

Childcare rocketed to political and media attention when the federal Task Force on Childcare, headed by University of Victoria sociologist Katie Cooke, released its report in 1986. The four-person Task Force had been commissioned by the Liberal government in Ottawa in May 1984. Its members included an eminent West Coast sociologist, an Ontario childcare expert, a Prairie law professor and a Quebecoise professor of economics. All four were sympathetic to women's issues and were officially non-partisan. The Task Force was given a far-reaching mandate to "examine and assess the need for childcare services and paid parental leave, as well as the adequacy of the current system in meeting this need" including making recommendations to the Minister Responsible for the Status of Women concerning the federal government's role in developing a system of quality childcare.

The relatively well-funded Cooke Task Force began the most comprehensive review of childcare services and funding ever undertaken in Canada. With an expert team of staff and researchers, the Task Force produced a 395-page final report and a six-part series of background research papers. Its findings ran the gamut. But its philosophic commitment was clear: "we have become convinced that sound childcare and parental leave policies can no longer be considered a frill, but rather, are fundamental support services needed by all families in Canada today."[1]

The Task Force discovered, from responses from over 7,000 parents and groups across the country and its independently commissioned research, that:

- nearly two million children 12-years-old and under have parents who work or study a substantial part of the week, but that there exist in Canada enough licensed daycare spaces for fewer than one tenth of them;
- more than 80% of Canadian children receive non-parental care in informal, unlicensed, unsupervised or unregulated settings;
- very little licensed childcare is available in rural areas, for immigrants, or for children whose parents work irregular hours;

---

1. Cooke, K. et al. 1986. *Report of the Task Force on Childcare.* Supply and Services Canada: Ottawa. p. xxiv.

- the number of single parents has doubled in the previous 20 years, until they now head up 11% all Canadian families;
- child-rearing is rapidly becoming economically prohibitive for parents, and "all the evidence points to a significant rise in voluntary childlessness in the years to come."

Out of facts like these the Task Force made some dramatic childcare proposals for a generous, massive and generally well-thought-out service for Canadian families. It laid out a series of recommendations to move in stages towards a universal and comprehensive childcare and parental-leave system by 2001. It said the government should start with a "good faith" grant to the provinces of $2 per day for ordinary child spaces (with $4 for infants or disabled children and $1 for after-school or half-day spaces). The federal government should then lay out additional money for five years to improve the current daycare system, making more spaces available and cutting costs to parents. Then it should agree to shoulder with the provinces half the daily expense of all daycare across the country with the goal that the daycare system would be universally available and publicly financed by the year 2001. Parental leave at a child's birth also should be extended within ten years from its present 17 weeks to 26.

The cost would be significant—about $6 billion annually. "The matter, in our view," the Task Force said with sensible logic, "is simply one of priorities, of determining which current programmes have a higher or lower priority than the care of our children and the future of our citizenry."[2] The proposed cost was obviously more than the Tories could stomach. The *Globe and Mail* summed it up for them by saying Katie Cooke's "prescriptions seem extraordinarily stiff."[3]

But the Task Force suggested ways of financing well within the reach of government. It pointed a finger at "a multitude of tax exemptions, tax deductions and tax credits that are both regressive—resulting in enormous tax saving to people with high incomes—and have the perverse effect of stimulating saving in a country that presently has one of the highest rates

---

2. Cooke, et al. 1986, p. 341.

3. March 11, 1986. *Globe and Mail.*

of saving in the industrial world."[4]

The Task Force got specific. It mentioned such things as the recently lowered corporate income tax rate, a move that in 1979 alone had cost the federal government a full $1 billion. Then there was the recent Tory tax exemption on $500,000 in capital gains over a lifetime, and the tax deductions for investment in retirement savings plans and in corporate oil and gas drilling funds. Were these the sort of things the government wanted to put ahead of "the care of our children and the future of our citizenry"?

The Special Parliamentary Committee

Research is time-consuming and reports take years. Thus, the Conservatives took federal office in 1984, during the main part of the Cooke Task Force's work. Even before the Cooke Task Force reported its findings, the Tories had begun a parallel investigation in the form of a Special Parliamentary Committee chaired by Conservative MP Shirley Martin. That Committee had a membership of politicians—four Tories, one Liberal, and one New Democrat—to "examine and report on the childcare needs of the Canadian family." What the Katie Cooke Task Force had begun was superseded with a crucial shift in focus. Instead of studying non-parental care or childcare in support of working women, the Special Committee led by Tory MP Shirley Martin would look at "the care of all kinds of children in all types of care situations."[5]

It was the Tory way of turning back from a clear focus on daycare and parental leave and toward a diffuse consideration of "family support."

The Special Committee visited 31 Canadian cities and towns and heard from 975 persons, including childcare advocate groups, commercial operators and anti-daycare groups of all kinds. Tories on the committee soon began to find confusion where the Katie Cooke Task Force had found agreement. In statements to the press, Tories on the Committee "indicated they didn't see a consensus in the deputations about daycare,"

---

4. Cooke, et al, 1986. p. 341.

5. Martin, 1987, p. 3.

said Tricia Willis, who was then a student of social work at the University of Toronto. "So we decided to find out."

She and two other researchers, Martha Friendly and Julie Mathien, put together a paper called "Childcare: What the Public Said" that methodically reviewed all 975 briefs. They found that the people who had addressed the Special Committee were clear about what they wanted. They overwhelmingly believed the effects of childcare on children and families to be beneficial. They wanted childcare to be universally accessible. They agreed that parents should pay some fees for childcare. They wanted a comprehensive childcare system as opposed to using public funds to encourage parents to stay at home. And they opposed giving public support to profit-making commercial childcare.

This last point, in fact, was most revealing. Half of all the people wanting public aid for profit-making childcare were themselves commercial daycare operators. Once you subtracted them from the total, only 11.5% supported aid to commercial, profit-making childcare. A full 77% opposed it.

Yet the Tories eventually came out in support of commercial childcare. This was one clear policy position the Tories were able to reach after finding that, in the words of the majority report of the Special Committee, the views expressed by the people were "so diverse (that) the Committee cannot report that there is a consensus among Canadians about how best to address the issues and solve the problems."[6]

The Child Care Act, Bill C-144, which the Tories eventually proposed—based largely on the Martin Committee—held none of the Katie Cooke recommendations.

Gone was the promise of universal daycare by the start of the century; gone was the initial "good faith" grant to the provinces; gone were the guidelines that the Katie Cooke Task Force had meticulously worked out; gone was the stipulation that all new funds be directed solely toward licensed non-profit daycare. And gone was the proposal to extend parental leave to 26 weeks, which had also been proposed by the Tories' own Special Committee. (The Tories did later extend parental leave

---

6. Martin, S. et al. 1987. *Sharing the Responsibility*. Report of the Special Committee on Childcare. p. 5.

to 25 weeks, however, by changing its Unemployment Insurance regulations, to take effect in 1990. But the government at the same time moved to stop making any government contributions to Unemployment Insurance, forcing employers and employees foot the whole bill.)[7]

The federal government ended up pledging instead, in Bill C–144, $3 billion spread out over seven years to create 200,000 new daycare spaces by 1995, plus $2.3 billion in tax assistance schemes. On the face of it, that sounded like a step forward. But childcare activists soon pointed out that the old Canada Assistance Plan, which is open-ended (it offers half of every dollar spent by the provinces for subsidized day-care) and whose childcare provisions the new bill would suspend, might have achieved that number of new spaces anyway by 1995.

One part of the Tory "childcare strategy" did go into effect under Jake Epp's direction. This was the move to put more money into the hands of individual parents through tax deductions and credits.

This category of Tory largess would amount to $2.3-billion over the next seven years—added onto the $1.7 billion that parents would already be receiving under provisions of previous Liberal schemes. The money was to be used in two ways: to boost from $200 to $484 a year the tax credit already given to poor or middle-income parents who care for their children at home or just don't have any receipts to show for daycare; and to raise the ceiling on income-tax deductions to $4,000 for parents who do have childcare receipts (the previous limit was $2,000).

Among those not impressed by the logic of this move were the members of a delegation from Kids First of Alberta. They offered the House Committee a tax breakdown to show that a married mother staying at home with two preschool children and husband out working could expect to get $523 back from the government, while a married mother and father in the same low-income bracket with outside jobs and two kids in daycare could expect subsidies of about $5,000. The Tories, obviously,

---

7. This expansion to 25 weeks pales somewhat in comparison to Sweden's decision the same year to extend its paid parental leave to 18 months by July, 1991.

weren't "supporting family choice," even though their stated aim was to offer tax breaks to individual families.

On the other hand, the Tory measures did hand over greater amounts to well-to-do families by boosting the income-tax deduction. Even the Tories' own Special Committee on childcare had advised the government to stop this deduction altogether because it was "widely perceived to be unfair." Under this scheme, the richer a family, the more government aid it got. But instead of stopping it, the Tories expanded it. It became increasingly obvious that the Tory "Childcare Strategy," which proposed to put a ceiling on CAP and to shift a large proportion of new federal money to tax deductions for parents, had more to do "with control and restructuring than supporting childcare."[8]

Midway through his deliberations on Bill C–144, after constant badgering by daycare advocates, Jake Epp realized he hadn't allotted enough money for even the promised 200,000 new spaces, so he added $1-billion to the pot.

Enriched with an extra billion dollars, the bill still met adamant opposition from daycare advocates at a hastily convened session of the House legislative committee. Petitioner after petitioner—in more than 20 deputations—compared it to the long-condemned Canada Assistance Plan, and found the Tory bill sadly lacking. "It is very embarrassing," Sharon Irwin of Nova Scotia told the Committee. "We have certainly preached against CAP for a long, long time. It is only because Bill C-144 (the Tory bill) places low- and middle-income subsidies and special needs entitlements at such a great risk that we are here today as defenders of that component of CAP.... (This bill) is not the generous act the federal government claims it to be."[9] "As a matter of fact," said Havi Echenberg, Executive Director of the National Anti-Poverty Organization, "I am quite sure CAP was not a great mechanism. But it had some protection for low-income people, and as far as we can see this bill has none."

---

8. Prentice, Susan. September 1988. "The 'Mainstreaming' of Daycare" in *Resources for Feminist Research*. p. 60.

9. From the transcript of the House Legislative committee hearings. Irwin spoke as a member of the board of the Canadian Day Care Advocacy Association.

Six hundred pages of official, bilingual minutes are filled with testimony from Sharon Irwin, Havi Echenberg and more than 20 other activists and groups, mainly daycare advocates and labour organizations, who pressed the House Committee for drastic changes to the bill in the late summer of 1988. The government finally refused to change its bill. It was junked only by the Tories calling the election of 1988. Throughout the election it was held up as the thing the Tories wanted to do. They won, but they never revived the bill.

Jake Epp said after winning the election that Bill C-144 was just fine, he saw nothing wrong with it, and he planned to send it back to Parliament just as it was.

But Epp was soon replaced in the Health and Welfare portfolio by former Defence Minister Perrin Beatty (later moved to Culture), who came on talking tough, and things looked even worse. "I don't think that we can cure all of our social and health-care problems through cheque-book prescriptions," he intoned in a luncheon speech a few weeks after his appointment.[10] Little was said about childcare in the subsequent Speech from the Throne. Childcare advocates, hoping for a new start, told Parliament in February 1989 they wanted no fewer than a million childcare spaces—five times the number that then existed—by the century's end. But curbing the federal deficit became the cause célèbre in Finance Minister Michael Wilson's budget announced that May, and daycare legislation was put off until closer to the next election in the 1990s.[11]

Confronting the Obstacles

The four central problems with the Tories' welfare approach to childcare were and are (1) bad funding, (2) a lack of quality guidelines, (3) the jeopardizing of assistance to the poor, and

---

10. *Globe and Mail*, February 3, 1989.

11. By June 1990, after the fall of the Meech Lake Accord, the Prime Minister's advisers were already commenting on the need for a "mid-mandate change" and a shift from the Tories astringent fiscal agenda to "a new, softer agenda [that] has to begin: childcare, the environment, job training and employment." See Graham Fraser, "PM's aides rethinking plans," *Globe and Mail*, June 30, 1990.

(4) the further commercialization of childcare throughout Canada.

The Tory bill was stingy. Everybody who opposed it agreed about that. But Tory tight-fistedness was nothing so simple as the mere unwillingness to offer public resources. Within that tight-fistedness was a clear ideological design. It not only sought to meet the public clamour for daycare—and win the 1988 federal election—by shifting only as much public wealth as necessary toward social services. It also determined to parcel out that money in an ideologically fitting way. So the problem with funding was not just scarcity of funds, but methods of distribution, and the terms under which that money would be allotted.

Take, for example, the Tory move to shift the preference given to daycare for the poor under the old Canada Assistance Plan. The old CAP was definitely an instrument of welfare. Daycare advocates had no love for daycare being seen as welfare at all; they wanted it designated as a public service open and free to all. But they saw the Tory bill knocking away the preference given to the poor—without holding out the hope of a universal service. As Lise Corbeil-Vincent, Executive Director of the Canadian Day Care Advocacy Association, described it: "There is no doubt that the bill as it stands impairs the funds traditionally allocated to low- and middle-income families and to special-needs children. It seems to me that the principle of 'do no harm,' which is an essential condition of this bill to be accepted, has not been respected."

Nearly all the petitioners against the bill criticized the Tory government's refusal to set federal guidelines. The "National Strategy on Child Care" set out by Cabinet had used a number of high-sounding words in its preamble, and Prime Minister Brian Mulroney had told the Commons the bill would establish "one of the most advanced childcare systems anywhere in the world." But the legislation itself made the federal government seem little more than tax-collector and distributor of funds to the provinces. The bill was all granting formulae and distribution mechanisms.

But in the very *lack* of direction was a direction that childcare advocates lamented. The government wanted to offer a laissez-faire deal to provinces that would support whatever childcare a province wanted to finance, with no strings attached. Advocates saw this as an abdication of federal responsibility. The post-war dream of a strong central state, with a commitment to equitable funding, universal access and portability of welfare services across the country went up in smoke. Instead of federal leadership, the Tory government proposed to be a junior cash-handler.

The lack of guidelines meant, for example, that children in Alberta could continue to be taken care of by 18-year-olds completely untrained for the job, and that Nova Scotia could keep allowing up to seven infants to be cared for all day long by a single adult. These substandard conditions, reprehensible to many parents and childcare workers and criticized by the Katie Cooke Task Force, were to be continued because the federal government refused to attach any strings to its money. And hidden in the aimlessness was the stipulation, as well, of letting federal money flow to commercial operators. The federal Tories were determined to protect free market "choices" through a hypocritical notion of respecting "consumer decisions."

Martha Friendly of the Childcare Resource and Research Unit in Toronto told the Parliamentary Committee the lack of guidelines "renders Bill C-144 ineffective as a piece of Canadian social legislation." And Don Aitken of the Alberta Federation of Labour said the bill "will only perpetuate nation-wide chaos in inequality in childcare." Being from Alberta, Aitken had a special cause to plead. His province's Conservative government, as he put it, "is firmly opposed to the basic concept of daycare," and Premier Donald Getty had set the tone "by insisting that a dichotomy exists between daycare and parental love and that they are mutually exclusive."

Opposition to lack of guidelines was not unanimous. Quebeckers stood opposed to any imposition of criteria. Lorraine Vaillancourt of the Quebec Federation of Labor, told the Committee. "We believe that the federal government's mandate is to provide funding and that we in Quebec will look after regulating our own standards." Quebeckers argued against federal standards, not to lower standards, but to gain self-determination.

On the issue of standards, aside from the matter of constitutional rights, advocates were united. The first consensus was the importance of developing a childcare system, not a piecemeal patchwork. A second key was opposition to giving federal money to private, profit-making daycare operators.

The Politics Of Childcare

We generally assume that politics are found in systems of government. But the more we take in the feminist perspective that "the personal is political," the clearer it is that there are politics everywhere. From the government's perspective, only childcare *policy* is political and childcare *services* are a mere service. But the truth is that politics are in childcare services themselves.

The philosophy which underlies a childcare programme is political. Take, for example, the question: Do parents, workers, children have a say in decision-making or does it rest with an owner or a bureaucracy? That's a political question. An answer must tackle questions of power, control, and representation. But there are other less obvious political questions that relate to programming, to pedagogy and to the socialization children experience. These are questions such as: Has a conscious effort been made to challenge gender-stereotyping or do boys do "boy things" while girls do "girl things"? Or: Are children taught noncompetitive games and cooperative conflict-resolution, or does the loudest and biggest child win? Or: Does the programme and staff reflect multiculturalism and anti-racist values, or do children grow up thinking that everyone is white, celebrates Christmas, and eats pork?

If there are politics in the simplest questions of programming and administration, then thinking about the political response to the childcare crisis demands that we address the micropolitics inside childcare programmes, including the politics of childcare research.

The politics of childcare services proposed by the Martin Special Parliamentary Committee were Tory through and through. But what about the politics of the Katie Cooke Task Force? Compared to the Special Committee, it was a revolutionary document. But what kind of politics of service did it propose?

The Katie Cooke Task Force offered Canadians a big picture of the gross inadequacy of public childcare arrangements in this country and proposed something magnificently new. To read it critically is not to deny the central importance of the project. But on matters of the struggle for home and community and of the love and dignity of children and women within these settings, the Task Force draws a large blank—perhaps because the government did not aim it in that direction. The closest it comes to mentioning the love and dignity of children is in a section called "Psycho-Social Needs," where it declares that children need, among other things, "love, compassion and understanding":

> Development of the capacity to be sensitive and responsive to the needs of others has its genesis in early life. A child who is wanted, accepted and valued for his/her own sake can develop a positive relationship with parents or substitutes, and in doing so, develop a positive image of him/herself.
>
> Children learn to love by first receiving love, compassion and understanding. In the early stages of development, children give little and receive a lot, because they are totally dependent on parents or substitutes. Gradually they learn to give, for example, by smiling. Later in life, the child learns to develop friendships and peer relationships.
>
> Nurturers must be cognizant of child development, and ensure through their attitudes and behaviour as they care for children that children's needs are understood and respected. Failure to meet the need for love, compassion and understanding can result in anger, hatred, lack of concern for others and inability to develop healthy personal relationships. This is outwardly expressed in acts of violence and delinquency.[12]

What could be more humane than to offer children love, compassion and understanding? But the question that goes begging is one of context: in what social setting, with what history and sense of place? And who are these children who

---

12. Cooke, et al, 1986. p. 64.

learn to love by first receiving love, compassion and understanding, who at first "give little and receive a lot"? Once these questions are raised, the curious quality of the prose in the Task Force report starts to make cool, logical sense.

The Task Force approach fits into what sociologist Margrit Eichler in another context describes as the too-typical social science approach to family studies in which "children are, at best, seen as individuals who have to be cared for, who need to be socialized, but not as people who may have divergent viewpoints as to what is happening within a particular family."[13] Children, she says, are often "seen as passive members being acted upon by their parents, not as active participants who themselves exert an influence on the adults they are dealing with as well as their siblings." Just as offensive is the notion that the family is fine, that all it needs are professional "supports." As we saw in Chapter 3, there are many relations which must be challenged before women, men and children can realize our longings for a just society and healthy families.

It is interesting to note that the Task Force declares that infants eventually do "learn to give, for example, by smiling." Babies smile, and their smiles are gifts. But that's probably the least of their early gifts, even though the most adaptive and highly lauded by adults. What do we do with all the other things? Like pooing or crying? "Nurturers," we are told, "should be cognizant of child development and ensure through their attitudes and behaviour as they care for children that children's needs are understood and respected." What is one to make of a language that denies the truth that it tries to say? How is a child to respond to care by "cognizant nurturers"?

The words speak in the voice of experts. There is no flow, no give-and-take in these prescriptions. The report's professional and scientific voice seems aimed at capturing and keeping rather than releasing and freeing. Thus, the power of the helping agencies is vaunted, and the powers of the local community of children and adults disparaged. This is perhaps a necessary foreclosure in the dispensing of governmental welfare.

What, then, does it communicate? It communicates a bur-

---

13. Eichler, M. 1988. *Families in Canada Today: Recent Changes and their Policy Consequences*. 2nd ed. Gage: Toronto.

eaucratic, non-social, a-historical grasp of who children and families are and how their needs are to be met. One comes away with a curiously cribbed view of human nature, where reality is styled to meet the proprieties of a larger system.

The trouble with the definitions of the Katie Cooke Task Force is not their imprecision but the assumption that childcare could be produced by the professional elite and put into force in a top-down, centrally controlled and administered system. It makes childcare into a production that can be quality-checked and delivered much like a mini-van off the line at Oshawa.

Childcare is something else, and the difference is critical. For one thing, childcare is a process more than a product. It is intimate and particular; it must be generated in community or it isn't what we wish to define as childcare at all.

It is a choice, as Susan Prentice has written elsewhere, between "care-as-commodity" and "care-as-social relations": "In the objectified language of social policy, quality of care is merely a technocratic manipulation of the professional standards of early childhood education. When the objective of childcare is understood as the safeguarding of children for 40 hours a week while their mothers work, the relations sustained and created by care are inconsequential when compared to the successful provision of adequate 'spaces.'" Reducing care to those terms keeps the vexing problems of sexism and class bias alive in childcare.[14]

To get beyond that expert-monopolized system, with its alienation from the community, we have to look first at language. How different are the stilted words of the Task Force from those of Fredelle Maynard, a parent and grandparent who wrote a book at about the same time called *The Childcare Crisis*.[15] "Do babies recognize their mothers?" Maynard writes. "At a surprisingly early age, they do. Or more precisely, they recognize the look, smell, sound and touch of a familiar caretaker, responding to familiarity as humans do, with relief and pleasure.... It now appears that newborns are to a surprising degree organized and competent. On the first day of life, they distinguish between regular milk and milk with corn syrup...."

---

14. Prentice, 1988. pp 59-63.
15. Maynard, F. 1986. *The Child Care Crisis*. Penguin: Toronto. p. 42.

These words flow from a person who has learned to take what children give. They recognize the physicality, the bodily essence of the child in all its messiness, brilliance and humanity.

The Task Force, describing the needs of the child, imposes its needs on the child it purports to describe. The needs of the Task Force are to create a childcare system that a federal government in a western democracy wedded to a capitalist economy and familiar with the philosophy of a welfare state, can administer. The child that it finds "in need" is a child that can be serviced by the government of that system. This entails defining children to fit the pattern into which they are to be drawn by the "helping" apparatus of a central state.

In this apparatus a lot can go wrong.

The Underside Of "Service"

It is no exaggeration to say that one of the centres we examined practised a regimen of verbal censure against children that was tantamount to brutality. Yet this took place under a veneer of civility that made the daycare workers into disciplinarians of sweet good reason.

Control was the overwhelming concern. This is not to say the 21 children, ages two-and-a-half to five, were cudgelled. "Discipline" doesn't usually work like that any more, although spanking is still practised in different parts of the country. Children in this centre were almost always spoken to in calm voices—told to sit down, to stand up, to be still, to quiet down, and so on, ad infinitum.

It went like this: Hal wanted to take off his sweatshirt—he said he was too hot. But he was helping a staffperson clean up the doll centre. "You can take that off as soon as you've finished cleaning up in here—you're too busy right now," the worker told him.

If children didn't obey, threats were made that food would not be served or that the child would be excluded from the group. The directives were arbitrary and random. A three-year-old wasn't supposed to squirm in his chair prior to snack-time, at which the children were about to have soda crackers, slices of pear, chunks of cheese and apple juice. The proper stance at this moment, with hunger at a high pitch, was total passivity. Tables of children that were "nice and quiet" were served first. And the cups were to be drunk from and not played with: "If you continue to play with those cups you're going to lose them," was a constant refrain.

At reading time an attendant packed 21 children into a carpeted corner bound by bookshelves. It took her some time to achieve a satisfactory state of quiet. Then a father came through the door with his child—late. The son clung to him in great sobs and tears until the father pried himself loose and strode out the door while another worker took the crying boy away from the group. He howled and sobbed. The reader kept reading from the book as if nothing else were happening, and the children listened miserably. Finally, the distressed boy joined the edge of the group.

At one point the children shouted in response to something the attendant read. "Tomas, Tomas," she said, singling out one of them. "I do not want you to show me with your voices." She went back to reading in a dispirited, disappointed tone. The children started babbling. "Children this is getting much too loud," she shouted. She mixed her reading with commands: "This is a B. B is for butterfly. Samuel, turn around. Tomas, why don't you go back and sit where you were before?" and so on, until the book was finally done, and she ended with, "How 'bout I start sending children who are quiet to the door?" which she did. They filed one by one to the door. Tomas was the last to be called.

As a way of control, the group was pitted against the individual. A child slow at putting on his boots was told that the others were irritated at having to wait for him. In fact the attendants themselves were making the others wait; they were the ones who were impatient, not the children.

The point in all this seemed not so much training in good behaviour as in self contempt, if one were to judge by attitude and actions alone. It was as if childhood had to be shamed out of these children. What was shown to be wrong was not so much hurting other children, or hurting one's self, as being one's irrepressible, bodily self—at age three. The children were being drilled in a tyranny aimed against their bodily urges, against spontaneity, against stepping over arbitrarily set lines. A three-year-old's defence in that setting had to be either complicity with the system against one's self or rebellion. There was no middle way.

This is not to say the children on their own would have been little angels. They sometimes hurt each other, they ridiculed the weak, they excluded one another—as well as showing a lot of generosity and kindness. But hurtful acts drew no more censure from the attendants than did getting out of line.

A child at a snack table, seemingly for no reason, gave off a sharp scream. "Do you want to leave the snack table, Erica?" an attendant called. "Why are you screaming?" The question was not answered; no answer was expected. Two children, one of them Erica, later started talking animatedly in good humour. A worker shushed them. She told them to raise their hands if they wanted juice.

The reprimands in this room were primarily aimed at one child—an Asian boy. His name rang out time and again. When friction broke out between him and another child, he usually got the blame. The other children had designated him as a trouble-maker and talked about him in those terms. Racial biases were actively reproduced. So were sexist notions about boys and girls. In a culture as steeped in competition, racism and sexism as ours, it is inevitable that these prejudices infect a programme—unless a conscious, thoughtful campaign ensures that equality and solidarity are the norm.

A director at another centre, when asked what the basic aim of the centre was, replied: "I think my primary goal would be to ensure that the children create a positive self-image." Others we talked to gave similar replies. The term "positive self-image" was a nagging question. Why was it a primary goal, and how was it taught? From observations at the centre we have just described, "positive self-image" seemed a ghastly joke. These children were being drilled in a contempt for their minds and bodies. To create a "positive self-image" on top of that would create an "image" terribly at odds with a child's true, if horribly perverted, feelings.

This concern about "positive self-image" seemed an artificial goal. If one's strengths, sex, culture, abilities and bodily powers were not seen as deeply evil, or inadequate until rebuilt in line with the system, why must early childhood educators worry about implanting in their little charges a "positive self-image"? It seemed a problem, not of children, but of system-trained adults.

Our early childhood education authorities surely don't mean to train workers to browbeat children. They are only keeping order, exerting "discipline," all of it "for the children's own good." Yet those methods are bound to split children away from themselves with a loathing for childhood that will cripple them throughout life—in ways that conform to societal norms of control, including public schooling. And they are so common to childcare as to be all but hidden from view. Our task, as Amy Rossiter suggested it in her remarkable book on early mothering, is to insist on the "Something" that we see in what our society declares to be "Nothing," especially in the sphere of childcare.[16] This includes seeing what is nonsense in common-sense.

It happens that the centre where the harsh "discipline" took place was not a "bad" school. It was not commercially run for profit. It was run by a community agency with parents on the board. Those in charge were professionally trained, and the centre operated within the guidelines set by Ontario's Day Nurseries Act. There was nothing illegal or substandard about it. Some of the parents said they were lucky to have such a fine centre.

Yet other places visited, also co-operative or non-profit, did not operate like that—at least not while one of us was there. So what distinguishes a good daycare model from a bad one, and how do government policies make a difference?

The ill-treatment of children clearly has roots in things deeper and more pervasive than funding shifts at Ottawa. Those roots lie in the inequities of modern society, in sex, race and class biases that undergird and permeate our institutions, including the family, and that will permeate daycare as well — unless we can find ways to confront them.

One cannot know the exact causes of the oppression in a

16. Rossiter, A. 1988. *From Public to Private: A Feminist Exploration of Early Mothering*. Toronto: Women's Press. p. 19.

childcare programme, but some factors are not hard to imagine. Consider the simple fact that the people in charge receive wages inadequate to the demands of their work, that they may foresee no personal advancement, that no community of support surrounds their efforts, that their homes are patriarchal and demeaning to women, that they may have been brought up in circumstances that did not recognize their gifts as children.

The childish clamour in this room of 21 children threatened to plunge the daycare workers into a state of isolation comparable to that of a mother at home with a single child. True, there were several adults at hand, but each of them seemed radically stranded with the kids. Amy Rossiter has pointed out how a mother's isolation with an infant can promote the damage it is supposed to prevent. An isolated adult, usually a mother, finds it necessary to train the infant to want less so that she can retain her adult identity, while standing vulnerable to the infant's demands. Something comparable seemed to be happening here: the intolerable isolation had not gone away. It had followed the children into daycare.

Insofar as "the personal is political," the vexing reproduction of race, sex and class biases must be addressed in daycare politics. We have to acknowledge them or we will have invented new forms around the same old injuries. We can have bad daycare with good funding. This happens—and will continue unchecked—if we fail to fight social oppression, alienation, and the curse of hierarchy and competition in local communities.

It is not only the children who need alternative, democratic politics of care. The parents who use the care, the workers who staff the programme, and the community of which they are all part of also need a broadly based self-conscious politics. We know how to begin to provide this alternative kind of childcare. There is a long history of community-based attempts to reshape childcare. And these strategies work: they're practical, reasonable and effective. It is to this alternative model of childcare that we now turn.

Chapter Seven

Organizing For The Future

Our approach to childcare might best be described as community childcare—care of, for, and by the community. It is about childcare taking place within community and as a way of building community, and of the community itself making the critical decisions about that care.

The proposition of community childcare—by no means a new idea in Canada—is also by no means utopian. It is a tough, realistic demand. And what is meant by community childcare is something quite precise and attainable; it can be directly fought for and won.

In spite of Tory foot-dragging, we are building a massive country-wide daycare system. The capitalist workforce—not just oppressed families—demands a childcare system. The question is: what is it going to look like? Privately owned or public? Profit-making or co-operative? And with what guidelines? How will children, parents, staff and the public be involved in this system? It is now or never for a "community" perspective.

If childcare is "in community"—as opposed to a mere service delivered by an agency or central government—what does that mean in actual practice? It certainly does include public assistance. But exactly how can the state—which is chacterized by the sectarian demands of politics and the larger imperative of maintaining the status quo—support community-based, high quality care?

We have to try not just to secure excellent daycare but also to win over the larger state and social institutions that must support that daycare. We can neither opt out of the state system nor give in to its divisive welfare-state priorities. Something new top-to-bottom must be created for the care of children. The struggle for this is part of the fight to make our state system more truly an expression of the people it represents.

The question comes down to this: will it be a democratic state, or will it be a state that fronts for corporate capital and imposes alien values through its agencies of control?

The Organizing Principle

An assumption of this book is that technology cannot be politically neutral, that the grant structures and organizational methods of any institution always impose political priorities on what happens at the level of care. The way a place is set up and financed will influence strongly what happens in daycare.

Jerome Bruner, a child psychologist who worked with childcare systems in both Britain and the United States, maintains that "there's nothing abstract about institutional climates." He says that how a place is set up is more or less how it will run—its micropolitics will express a larger political vision. Bruner found a striking difference between centres depending on the organizing principle. "... There is very little question that a nursery's pervasive style is strongly affected by the institutional objectives they early choose or fall into.... A respect for children's problems and collegial mutual respect in the staff are built into the *modus vivendi* of the nursery at the time the nursery is established."

He adds: "It is worth a long pause for reflection at the very start to make clear just what ends people have in mind in coming together to set up a nursery altogether."[1] What is true of the individual centre is all the more true of a national daycare system. And a crucial factor in being clear about "what ends people have in mind" is to allow and promote democratic decision-making at the grass-roots, where the establishment of daycare should take place.

---

1. Bruner, Jerome. 1980. *Under Five in Britain*, Grant McIntyre: London. pp. 164, 167.

Our ability to change the nature of state services depends partly on the links we build between the producers and the users of those services. That's where love and power must come together in a forceful way. Childcare workers and parents can be—need to be—allied in the cause of good childcare. Top-down, professsional and bureaucratic governmental measures won't work unless they meet the priorities set by the community.

The groundwork for this approach has been laid. We know, in part, what a community approach means in practice from the activities of daycare activists during the 1960s and 70s, and to some extent, the 80s.

But our traditional ways of building "community" are faltering. Many long-time activists, committed to the principles and politics of alternative, community-based childcare, have simply burned out. The high personal cost of exhaustion is too much. Confronted with the choice of a bureaucratic state on the one hand and a menacing free-enterprise childcare lobby on the other, many advocates have wearily agreed that the welfare state would do a better job than McBaby Skools. Many daycare workers long for the respectability, job security and decent wages of the education system. Tired of piecing together private solutions, parents want to see a reliable and standardized system of care. Many community activists have run low on steam in terms of building more "community" childcare on their own—their organizations are strapped for money, they are tired, and they know that the rapidly rising demand for daycare far outdistances their meagre resources. Many of them are spending much of their time getting even a small portion of the liberal "welfare/service" vision in place, twisting provincial and federal arms, and now pushing municipalities and school boards to help fill the enormous gaps.

But at the centre of this community experience, whether clearly articulated or not, has been an understanding that children give and receive, and that this human activity can be recognized at the core of good childcare. We can insist that public childcare provide what is needed to enable children, parents and childcare workers to exchange their gifts—to make community care possible. There are ways to rationalize the labour, to extend the best of our community-based experience in new and less fatiguing ways.

The words we find will have to transcend that false chasm between public and private, the pseudo-opposition between the family and the larger world. We must resist the common-sense idea that "quality" and "quantity" are opposites, or that childcare is *either* a mass service, *or* a community-based alternative. We must insist, always, on the whole nine yards: quality, quantity, and democracy for children, parents, workers and community.

This chapter explores the kind of daycare we can win if we organize.

Rearranging Work and Homes

The first requirement for a new vision of childcare is a rearrangment of the worlds of work. We need to change the relationship of women and men to both paid and unpaid work.

In the world of paid work, we need a shorter working day with more flexible hours, to allow adults and children more time together. As long as the market economy demands most of our time and energy, all the rest of life limps along on leftovers. The shorter working day is for every worker, not just a "mummy track" for women. It goes without saying that this shorter working day does not justify reduced wages, benefits or access to promotion.

We also need to ensure that women and men have equal access to job training and development, including equal pay for equal work, and good family leave benefits (including fully-paid parental leaves for birth or adoption, leaves for domestic responsibilities, time off with sick children and/or other dependents, etc.). Part of this will also involve an adequate system of social benefits to permit parents and caregivers who are not in the labour force—either temporarily or longer term—to enjoy a decent standard of living on public support.

We also need to extend the options of home life, so that households aren't only made up of nuclear couples and their children. Communities can be widened so that children and adults are in closer networks of support. This involves finding ways to encourage meaningful relations between adults and children who are not related: breaking down the walls between parents and non-parents. This would especially benefit gay and lesbian families, who currently aren't recognized as legitimate parents (partly because of that weary old common-sense about "blood being thicker than water"). Many other adults might choose to involve themselves with children if the nuclear family weren't so closed.

Decent Funding

Without the material resources, the best will in the world will fail. At base, we must find financing for high quality, universally accessible, free childcare. How could we fund childcare decently in Canada?

As far as federal financing is concerned, the Canadian Day Care Advocacy Association has offered a proposal: that the federal government offer the provinces a conditional grant of a fixed sum—in 1986 it was $5 a day—for every licensed childcare space. The CDCAA stipulates that this money go only to non-profit centres, and to commercial centres intending to become non-profit over a three-year transition period. Large chain-operated centres would not be eligible for funding.

The CDCAA also asks the government for a flat rate per capita grant of $25 a year for each child under 12 to be spent on daycare or related services by the provinces and territories. Local groups would decide with the provinces how to use the money, but it, too, would stay in non-profit hands.

One problem with these proposals is that they don't bind the provinces and territories to do their fair share for daycare. So a cost-sharing scheme could also be devised—similar to the old Canada Assistance Plan, which hooks federal aid onto provincial aid on a 50-50 basis. But 50-50 might not be everywhere equitable; some provinces are more wealthy than others, so regional adjustments in cost-sharing would have to be made.

All of this was worked out schematically with several possible options in a background paper for the Katie Cooke Task Force.[2] It shows that federal financing could be a lot simpler

2. Stotsky, Karen, "An Overview of Some Federal-Provincial Fiscal Arrangements and Proposed Options for Financing a System of Child Care in Canada" Series 2, *Financing Child Care: Future Arrangements, a background paper for the Report of the Task Force on Child Care* (Ottawa: Status of Women Canada) pp. 83–104.

than it is at present, and get the job done a lot better. To do this, governments must confront the mixed motives that come into play in existing funding schemes.

Community-Based Democracy

Childcare programmes should be governed by the people they serve. People affected by decisions must be the people who make the decisions. We need to ensure that parents, workers, children and community are fairly represented in decision-making.

Parents are central to childcare. We cannot permit daycare operate as if parents were essential only for delivering the kids and paying the bills.

Staff are central to childcare. We need a system of childcare which provides good working conditions, fair remuneration and benefits—including decision-making input and control. Childcare programmes can be models for alternative, democratic and cooperative workplaces.

Children, too, need appropriate input into the quality and experience of their days in care.

And, since childcare is about extending community relations, we need some way to integrate the broader community through outreach and participation.

But let's focus here on parent involvement. We've already pointed out that commercial childcare is, generally speaking, of poorer quality. A second, often hidden, variable to programme quality: parent involvement. The scientific research shows that parent-involvement is directly related to programme quality. One study of 431 full-day daycare centres by Ontario's Ministry of Community and Social Services showed that among the non-profit centres, those with parental involvement did the best job with the children. (Recall that not every non-profit daycare programme has a democratic decision-making structure. A directly-operated programme, for example, or a workplace centre operated as a division of a business may be "non-profit," but not community-based.)

Leslie Fruman, reporting on these findings in the *Toronto Star*, wrote that "the non-profit centres without parent involvement did not do as well. These included centres run by churches and by operators who appointed their own boards of directors, not including parents."[3] The study found, for example, that while 54% of the commercial operators and 45% of the church-run centres fell short of the Day Nurseries Act requirements on staffing, only 15% of the parent-run centres violated the Act. The involvement of parents in itself made a major difference because parents insisted on the centres being adequately staffed.

If parental involvement helps produce superior childcare, it also runs into a lot of problems of administration. A childcare centre's budget may run to half a million dollars; most parents are unqualified to handle the accounting and legal matters that this entails. "It's no longer your little co-op," commented Janet Davis, who helps co-ordinate daycare programmes in Toronto schools, "I mean these are big operations. They don't have the kind of expertise that they need sometimes to make the decisions that they have to make." Instead of blaming parents for lack of expertise, the Board decided to provide training. It started a series of workshops for parents and offered legal and financial advisers free of cost.

Even with assistance, parent involvement is never easy. A major problem, aside from lack of skills, is lack of continuity. Parents may well be intensively involved in daycare for the years while their children are passing through, but "drop out" once their children are six or seven. So parental daycare boards have to constantly orient newcomers to the work of running a centre. The staff, of course, may be on the board of directors as well, but parental support still varies greatly as parents come and go.

In communities where parents do not want to shoulder the task of sitting on local boards of directors, public administrators can be assigned to start daycare centres anyway—provided enough parents want them. Already a group known in Metro Toronto as Direction 2000, in agreement with the province, has volunteered to hold licenses for newly started centres until a community group can organize to take it over. That group has helped to train parents for the job of running centres. In that way children can be served in communities where parents won't or can't serve on committees. This help

---

3. Fruman, Leslie, *Toronto Star*, June 6, 1988, p. A16.

offered by Direction 2000 is an example of what could be done on a larger scale with public money, working toward universal access to childcare under local community guidance as quickly as possible.

We can develop models with clear mechanisms to balance direct control and responsibility by the people who are affected on a daily level, with the public responsibility.

Should Parents Pay Fees?

A major issue in funding childcare is whether or not it should be free of cost, or based on ability to pay. The judgment obviously depends in part on the priorities you make for other areas of government spending and the fairness of the tax system in place. There is little consensus on this question. As an end goal, we don't support parent fees: we advocate a system which is "free" at the point of delivery—paid for through a fair system of taxation and public support. Only a free system can prevent a two-tiered development of childcare with excellent care for the rich and custodial care for the poor. But we should review the debate on this question.

A study of 336 parents conducted for the Katie Cooke Task Force found 81% saying that parents should pay by ability on a sliding scale; only 10% thought childcare should be free to all, and only 8% thought parents should pay all costs.[4] A general poll of Canadian citizens taken by Decima Research in 1987 found 57% saying the primary responsibility for paying for daycare falls to parents; only 29% said it should be left to the government.[5]

Part of the reasoning for asking people to pay according to their ability is that the money represents an output of energy likely to be accompanied by a sense of having a say in what goes on at the daycare. In fact, judging by the Katie Cooke Task Force study, parents don't just think "government should

---

4. Lero, Donna S., et al. "Parents' Needs, Preferences, and Concerns About Child Care: Case Studies of 336 Canadian Families," Series 5 *Child Care Needs of Parents and Families, a support document for the Report of the Task Force on Child Care* (Ottawa: Status of Women Canada, 1985) pp. 23–112

5. Fillion, Kate. January 1989. "The Daycare Decision" *Saturday Night*, p.27.

do it." Parents think *parents* should do it, with childcare workers and public support. Of the 336 parents asked about who should look after the quality of childcare, the largest percentage (42.3%) said primarily parents. Almost as many, however, said responsibility should be shared by parents, providers, and government. It is a reasonable collaboration.

This notion that one only has control over things for which one pays, however, is too restrictive and easily blends with the market mentality. It may be true that a parent feels she has more rights to control and input if she is a "paying customer." But is that a model of social accountability which we want to base our future on?

As long as parent fees remain, however, a sliding scale seems the fairest way to set them. This may not be far different from the income and means test at present given under the Canada Assistance Plan to those who seek subsidies, except that it would be extended to all parents with children in the system. The basic principle would be that each family pay a portion of total costs according to its ability. Regions could be expected to require differing amounts of support from families, depending on the general living expenses of each region. The ground rule would be that no child would be excluded from a publicly funded, non-profit daycare provision, and parents would have a free choice as to their children's degree of involvement, with the fee adjusted accordingly.

Provision should also be made to assist parents who choose to care for their children at home, whether because of lack of daycare availability, inability of parents to find outside work, or simply personal choice. This assistance too could be regulated on a sliding scale based on need. Many parents prefer to stay home with infants or toddlers, instead of using licensed childcare.[6] This choice should be respected. Parents should not be coerced by economic pressure into going back to work until they are ready: hence we need a good system of parental leave

---

6. Maynard, F. 1985, *The Child Care Crisis*. Penguin: Markham Ontario. pp. 42–57. Another review of the research literature on the issue was prepared by Steen B. Esbensen in "The Effects of Day Care on Children, Families and Communities: A Review of the Research Findings," Series 3, *Child Care: Standards and Quality, a background paper for the Report of the Task Force on Child Care*, (Ottawa: Status of Women Canada, 1986) pp. 187–249.

to round out licensed childcare. A choice to take parental leave should not result in penalties or discrimination at tax time.

The Katie Cooke Task Force estimated governmental costs of providing the essential daycare needed by Canadian children in 2001—assuming no parental fees—to be on the order of $6.3 billion. It found the 1984 government spending on childcare to be a mere fraction of this, about $542 million. The Task Force proposed a sensible staging of these increased costs, starting with $116 million in the first year, working up to $6.3 billion by the year 2001, with a tax recovery of $600 million from new jobs, and with employers and employees supporting parental benefits through Unemployment Insurance premiums.[7]

Whatever the cost to taxpayers, we must, if serious about universal public daycare, work past the stage of parental fees. Childcare—like healthcare or education—is a fundamental part of what a democratic society offers to its members. No cash need change hands in a school or a hospital and no cash should change hands in a childcare programme, either.

Finding the funding is only one of the major issues in dealing with the question of publicly funded childcare in Canada. A deeper and more important concern is the way we want to bring up our children. What kind of childcare do we want to have with the money we get? What does it mean to raise children collectively, and what choices do we have in working this out together?

The Neighbourhood Hub

A group of activists in the Day Care Research Group worked out an option in the 1970s and early 80s that has been much discussed. It picked up many of the ideas that had been explored in cooperative and municipal daycare centres and drew them together in what was called the "Hub Model." It proposes a neighbourhood resource centre as a "hub" containing a daycare centre with flexible hours, affiliated with a range of supportive services and programmemes. These can include health care, parental education programmes, a drop-in centre, a

---

7. Cooke, 1986, pp. 339–340.

half-day nursery school, and a toy-lending service, heritage language and cultural celebrations, overnight care, programmes for sick or needy children, parent support groups, and other appropriate community services.

Radiating out from the hub would be assistance to other kinds of childcare, including work-place care, over-night care for shift-workers, emergency care for sick children, supervised private home care, and parental care at home.

The beauty of this model is that it enables an entire community of adults to be in touch with one another around the children. It creates a resource open to whatever kinds of childcare the parents and other providers needed; it is non-compulsory yet with no one excluded—all would have the share they wanted in the community venture. In cases of emergency or special need, different parts of the community would stand in for each other.

The hub model allows care-givers in private homes to have employee status with benefits, adequate salaries and the chance of further education. They would be part of a community that breaks down the isolation they often feel in present circumstances, working as they do in a grey market without full disclosure of pay received. And children in private home care could visit the centre for special events and take part in field trips. "The ideal structure," writes Nancy Miller Chenier in describing this plan, "would allow shared worker/parent control of care situations, and greater participation in decision-making."[8]

This could be a big step toward the refocusing of childcare that Urie Bronfenbrenner found necessary when he wrote *The Ecology of Human Development* in 1979. "In the past," he wrote, "such programmes were primarily child-centred, age-segregated, time-bound, self-centred, and focused on the trained professional as the powerful direct agent of intervention with the child."[9] The hub model offers to replace that with

---

8. Chenier, Nancy Miller and Helene Blais Bates, "The Informal Child Care Market: Public Policy for Private Homes" Series 3, *Child Care: Standards and Quality, a background paper for the Report of the Task Force on Child Care*, (Ottawa: Status of Women Canada, 1986) p. 175.

9. Bronfenbenner, Urie. 1979. *The Ecology of Human Development*, (Cambridge: Harvard University Press, 1979). Cited by Nancy Miller Chenier, above.

a community- and family-centred model, and to use the child's natural social group of parents, relatives, neighbours, and school personnel as the setting for care.

The information and resource centre included in such hubs is of great benefit to both parents and care-givers, as Chenier suggests: "It could be geared to the needs of a variety of parents—unwed, separated/divorced, teenage or older parents. It could increase parents' ability to assess quality of care-givers and care environments, thereby reducing anxiety. It could discourage socio-economic segregation and categorization.... The service must be seen by the community as open to disadvantaged or minority groups, as non-judgmental and non-threatening, and as heterogeneous in composition."

Chenier quotes psychologist Alicia Lieberman to make the point that public money put to use in this way for the self-help of communities is not poorly spent—not, at any rate, if what government wants to do is help people help themselves. "Paying middle-class professionals to help the poor might... perpetuate the myth of incompetence and justify a continued failure to act to change objective conditions. Paying the poor directly in a context that allows them to help themselves might be a first step toward acknowledging their human dignity and giving them a chance for self-reliance."[10]

Unloading Infrastructure

One way that governments need to assist local centres is by taking off their shoulders the burden of "infrastructure" matters. This would allow governments to assist the hub without dictating the policies of each centre. To run a childcare centre, parents and workers need an accounting service, legal assistance, janitorial service, and a warm, light, well-ventilated, draft-free building with good access, if possible, to a play space outdoors. This is a realm where "service" makes sense.

If "community care" is not to become a euphemism for government neglect, lay persons in these fields shouldn't have to carry the whole burden, even though they ought to give overall

---
10. Lieberman, A. Autumn, 1978. "Psychology and Day Care," *Social Research*, pp. 416–451.

direction to it. Parents and childcare workers loaded down with administrivia soon start to think community-based care is just too labour-intensive to be practical. But the choice isn't really between 100% do-it-yourself community care and a 100% professional-monopoly. The cooperative ground rests in letting the community have power and democratic control, while supporting it with publicly provided services. At least one major board of education has moved to offer accounting and legal services to daycare groups using space in its schools. Janitorial service, too, has been offered by many public bodies without charge. This provides a platform upon which parent/worker groups can—if they choose—get down to the delicate work of deciding together how to build a place for children.

Hassling out what a local daycare centre or hub will be like is the price of relevant childcare. There is little point in pining for more democratic structures unless we take the opportunity to create them. Parents need certain things for their children that others have a responsibility to help provide, and that's basis enough for trying to work things out democratically.

Hubs and Schools

Another hope for universal care has focused on the school system. It is ideally situated. It has buildings in the community richly adapted to children. It already has a modicum of local control through school boards, and it knows something about children and learning. In several cities, school boards already offer space for nominal fees to daycare groups, and Quebec has made school-age daycare part of its school provisions, although the funding comes from another provincial ministry than education.

There may be many advantages to school-run daycare. Its promoters point out that it can integrate a child's care from infancy through Grade 8, reducing the number of jarring shifts children endure in moving from system to system. Further, if daycare workers were part of that system they could organize within the teacher federations to push for decent salaries and reasonable working conditions. School systems, standing in for children of all ages, can be a powerful lobby for the needs of children of all ages. Most important, public schools seem the quickest possible route to universality and the surest bulwark against the spread of commercial daycare since there are no fees. All children have an unquestioned right to education.

Many daycare advocates see the neglected state of daycare as being similar to that of public education 130 years ago. They hope daycare will one day find acceptance as a universal public service as public education has done. But that requires critical thinking so that the contradictions that afflict public schooling are not reproduced.

Public school systems in Canada, as is evident in the history of their evolution, have long imposed middle-class values and norms, along with racial and gender biases. School systems still don't have an enviable record in educating working-class children. They've put too much effort into fitting children into the dominant social hierarchy and not enough into basic education. And what about the school bureaucracy already in place? In many cases it is an elitist and privileged structure, working by rigid patriarchal norms, in unquestioning service to a class-biased society; it is an administration that confuses its own survival and expansion with the well-being of children. The school bureaucracy of English Canada was set up as a mechanism of social control, as Alison Prentice points out in *The School Promoters*, and it has fulfilled that task with increasing sophistication down through the years.[11]

It is important to know that the early school promoters were not primarily interested in educational skills; they were interested in moral character, which translated into an appreciation of middle-class values and the centralized state control of learning. Much had to be destroyed in local communities for the centralized state to establish its norms of education; it forms an often ugly history that is only lately being brought to

---

11. Prentice, Alison. 1977. *The School Promoters: Education and Social Class in Mid-Nineteenth Century Upper Canada*, (Toronto: McClelland and Stewart) p. 183–184.

light.[12] Local communities need to be aware of this history as they make league with public education for the care of the very young.

Yet to their credit, public school educators also have opened up to parents who pressed for better service, more parental involvement, more flexible programmes and different approaches to learning in the past two decades. School systems do have elected school boards who try to respond to local demands, even though they are held in check by central provincial regulations and funding mechanisms. The alternative schools that sprang up under the guidance of parents and teachers may offer a model for daycare governance. They have in some cases involved parents intimately in school operations and adapted the programmes to special needs.

The hub model could be instituted through the public school as well as anywhere if parents, childcare workers, teachers and school board members took a mind to press for it. Each centre would require a local board including parents, daycare workers, teachers and the school principal; they would work out its philosophy, set up the rooms, hire the staff, set the hours and make the centre known to other parents in the community. This would require provinces to open the schools to children of all ages. Ontario has made a few steps in this direction by lowering the permissible half-day kindergarten age from 4 to 3 and by requiring that all new school buildings include space for daycare.

Using the school system to provide childcare requires thinking out problems of democratic control and decision-making. The Toronto Board of Education, which requires a majority of

---

12. See Bruce Curtis, *Building the Educational State: Canada West, 1836–1871*, (London, Ontario: Althouse, 1988). Curtis notes on page 143, after extensive documentation, "The central office sought to abolish the traditional powers of the local school meeting to decide almost all matters of educational import." On page 102, Curtis analyses the educational philosophy of Egerton Ryerson, the chief founder of the modern school system. Curtis writes: "Education was centrally concerned with the making of political subjects, with *subjectification*. But these political subjects were not seen as self creating. They were made by their governors after the image of an easily governed population. This was a different version of what other writers called the creation of 'willing and cheerful' obedience. Self government was social subordination."

parents on centre boards that use its schools, also allows teachers, as well as non-parent residents, to sit on the boards.

Such boards of directors would be in charge of practical matters, such as setting the centre's hours, selecting staff members, deciding on location and co-ordinating the programme with other institutions involving the children. They would also need to spend a lot of time at the beginning and at annual meetings, thinking through the basic philosophy of the centre and its affiliated services.

The staff could be hired from a reservoir of applicants certified by the larger school system; their salaries would be paid not directly by the local boards but by the larger system—in this case the school board—for two reasons: so that conflict over salaries would not split parents and workers, and so that the workers themselves could organized broadly to press for decent wages from the responsible government body.

Guidelines for Child Care

The core propositions being made here about childcare—that it take place in a community of giving and receiving, that it enable children to build trust and develop their selves in security, without the intrusions of class-bias, divisions of gender, race and commercial exploitation—need to be worked out openly and publicly. We will suggest here some of the guidelines we think need to be kept in mind as the groundwork for local discussions, as well as service planning on the part of governments.

Start at the elemental level of children's need for security. This goes well beyond mere physical safety and includes freedom from manipulation. Ontario's "Standards for Day Nurseries Services" required that "programmes should build in each child... a *feeling of being secure*." (Our italics.) The primary point here seems not to be that the child be *made* secure; the primary point is that the child be made to *feel* that way. This tiny shift of focus springs from the ideology of individualism at the root of liberal childcare systems. Aside from having security and acceptance—which seem recognized as necessary—children are to be made to feel that they have it. This locates the critical point inside the child instead of in the larger human environment. In practice, it can easily work out to an enlistment of mind control as an instrument of care; one of the daycare centres in Toronto is called Happy Faces.

This shift of focus can subtly undercut a child's security. If the child's feelings themselves become the focus of an orchestrated effort, the child's assertion of the self is endangered. In a truly democratic setting a child must be free to feel secure or insecure, as the case may be, while adults take the responsibility to create an environment that is actually secure.

Another basic security is freedom from exploitation. The point of exploitation is to extort from children what should not be taken from them or to manipulate them for ulterior purposes. Childcare in our country takes place in a society that lauds competition and condones exploitation as essential to human advancement. Laws have been made against child exploitation in its many guises, not merely, as in the 19th Century, against their exploitation in factories and mines. Now the laws quite rightly include prohibitions on forms of advertising that exploit children, because many powerful corporations would gladly do so and continue to do so despite the laws.

But we must go further to prevent the ravages of class, race and sexual prejudice. All children, of all classes, cultures, languages, abilities, sexes and nationalities—just like all adults—must be seen as lovable, worthy and equally important.

Of course, daycare workers need progressive training and support to help ensure that childcare programmes are respectful nurturing places. It is hard, slow, painful work to unlearn racism, sexism and prejudice and to confront it inside and outside a programme. This is a personal fight, but at a deep level the problem is also political and structural—in daycare as in the family.

The Adult Presence

The positive side of the task of building trust has to do largely with offering a plenitude and consistency of adult presence that enables the child to expand and grow without danger or threat. This is not a simple thing; we do not wish to deny its complexity here in singling out a few crucial issues. Childcare that enables trust to grow between children and between children and adults is a many-layered process.

The separation of private and public realms is shaken by daycare, because the gathering of children with adults in a community setting throws them into a public space and throws open their individual private relationships. The family is re-extended. There may well be an impetus within society to push daycare into a "female ghetto" and thus to shut it into a new quasi-private domestic space. But in fact it is also a public space.

A public daycare centre can be seen as an extension of love and solidarity in the larger society, and an extension of the larger society into the intimate sphere of the family. It is both at the same time, so it is in a sense a new realm. This social space has not existed before on a mass scale. It is neither wholly private nor wholly public, yet both private and public issues and concerns pervade childcare all the time.

As a public place, it also includes demands for privacy and intimacy that need to be respected. A child's most intimate activities—learning to use the potty, taking the first step, speaking the first word—will be happening for more and more youngsters outside the home, in a "public" environment that must also be "domestic." The ability of a daycare centre to let the two worlds of private and public—which traditionally have been split also into female and male—intermingle in creative ways will be a large element in their success. Important to this are the practical questions of the size of children's groupings and an adequate adult presence.

Children need the presence of adults. The adults who work with children need the support of other adults, too. Provinces have set out in their daycare regulations the outer limits of numbers of children to adults (the adult/child ratio) and the maximum number of children who can be kept in groups for long periods. These, as we have indicated, vary widely depending on the age of the child. Generally speaking, one adult is currently required for every three infants, and one adult for every seven or eight preschoolers.

Since staffing is the big cost in daycare, this is an area where daycare centres can play tricks with numbers to cut costs. It's easy enough to throw children together when a worker gets ill rather than to hire a replacement. Lunch breaks and coffee breaks often leave children lacking an adult presence. Childcare advocates emphasize that the provincial adult/child ratios are the outer limits, yet in profit-making systems and where programmes are strapped for cash, they become at best the norm.

What's the point of these legal limits? The point is to make sure nobody abuses children unduly by packing them in so as to either make or save money. The point of all the regulations, when it comes down to it, is to protect children from the carelessness or avarice of adults who either do not know better or would abuse children if not held liable to penalty.

This is the punishment model which we discussed in Chapter 4. Those external rules are required, but as shown at community-run daycares in the past, parents do view such rules as minimums and do not, as a general practice, try to go beneath them to scrape by with their children. We wouldn't throw out the outside standards, centrally established, for good childcare; in fact, in some cases, they need to be tightened. There always has to be an involvement of general, overall standards while government pays the bills. We hope that in a revised model of childcare, standards would no longer define the criteria for care. But finally, that would depend on a community's desire for its children.

Rich Play

We need to look at childcare with other eyes. Jerome Bruner tried to do this in an elaborate study of childcare in England. He took for granted that the main thing—and the most important thing—that happens in daycare is play. And then he asked a simple question: What produces "rich" play? The answers he found provide a few clues about good childcare.

By "rich" Bruner meant play that produces extensive talk, and that involves concentration over time. He found children do this best in small groups, especially in the presence of an adult. "Richer dialogue seems to require more intimate and continuous settings than most preschools now provide," he commented.[13] What often got in the way of rich dialogue

---

13. Bruner, 1980, p. 62.

between adults and children was what he termed the "management duties" of adults, which included their having to keep order.

The higher the adult presence, he found, the more extensive and elaborated was children's play and the more talk there was between adults and children. This may seem perfectly reasonable, but it sometimes takes research to show us what we know.

The National Day Care Study in the United States also found that in groups where the absolute number of children was small, children were more cooperative and responsive to the initiatives of adults and other children. They were more likely to engage in spontaneous talk and creative activity. They were less likely to wander aimlessly. Larger groups fared worse on all these scores. Neither more formal education by daycare workers nor adding more workers diminished the negative effect of large groupings of children.[14]

Scarcity is a great schoolmaster; if there is not enough "teacher" to go around, say, in a kindergarten class of 28, so that she has to resort to bells, gongs and other odd routines and punishments, those routines and punishments are what will have been learned. Scarcity will have done its duty as an educational device. The alternative is to let things descend into chaos where children hurt each other. But that is a bogus choice forced by the imposition of scarcity. That's how systems for the care and education of children make "necessary" the mind-numbing routines that teachers are then accused of imposing.

Scarcity—of either material or human resources—must not be used against the deserved richness of childhood. There is no excuse for it; our society is rich enough.

Good Workplaces

Children need someone to engage them with consistency and love. They need adults who just plain *like* them and are reliable—a small group of people on whom they can depend. This used to be almost exclusively the mother. Many critics of daycare have long held that taking the child away from the mother

---

14. Roupp, R. et al., *Children at the Centre*, final report of the National Day Care Study, Vol. I (Cambridge: Abt Books, 1979).

too early for too long can hurt the child irremediably. This may be true for some children and not true for others. Most of the research on child development has been steeped in sexism and gender bias, so it is difficult to be sure what children really need on this point. Some research suggests that most young children do not require a relationship exclusively with one person. In fact, as Amy Rossiter points out, being isolated with one other person can harm both child and mother.[15] But small children do need consistent care. They need the opportunity to relate to a small group of people over time. Certain people must be there for them. Frequent staff changes hurt children.

Since the daycare centre is where children are apt to spend many hours—over 8,000, according to one authority—the people at that centre are, next to the parents, ultimately important in all sorts of ways.[16] To build cooperative and happy partnerships with workers and parents, means that daycares must be good workplaces.

It starts with worker training and extends on all the way to wages, benefits and the elusive factors of respect and control over decision-making and relations with co-workers.

Studies show that formal training of workers improves the quality of the care offered, according to the conventional standards of quality. Simply the fact that they have any training at all in childcare methods improves workers' ability to deal with children, though workers always add the caveat that some people are "naturals" regardless of training.[17] The training needs to be much more than mere educational psychology; it needs to offer a vision of childcare as a process of giving and receiving, and to situate it firmly in the community context.

The Katie Cooke Task Force lists training as its third "indi-

---

15. Rossiter, Amy, *From Private to Public: A Feminist Exploration of Early Mothering*, (Toronto: Women's Press, 1988), Chapter 6, "Isolation," pp. 241–267.

16. Jerome Kagan, child psychologist, points out that the daycare of a child starting at six months and continuing to the sixth year has more than 8,000 hours "to teach him values, beliefs and behaviours and, potentially, is an enormously powerful influence over what that child will become." Quoted by Fredelle Maynard in *The Child Care Crisis*, (Markham, Ontario: Penguin, 1985) p. 136.

17. Cooke, 1986, p. 130.

cator of quality." The Task Force focuses on education as a tool in the early prevention of problems and the development of skills for relating to parents. Those are no doubt needed and well provided already by most colleges and schools. The vision of daycare as a democratic effort on the part of workers with parents and community would greatly broaden and strengthen its appeal.

One largely unnoticed trouble with daycare throughout Canada is the turnover of staff. The reasons for it are chiefly that the staff are underpaid and undervalued, which are not necessarily the same thing. The Katie Cooke Task Force found that in licensed centres—the best in the daycare business— 61% of the staff had been at their current centres for less than a year. And among care-givers in licensed family homes, over half had been in their current jobs for fewer than three years.[18] As these statistics show, daycare children are forced to adjust not only to daycare, but to frequent departures and arrivals within daycare. It is hardly a situation that fosters trust.

Low wages have forced many workers to hop from centre to centre in search of financial security and better working conditions. The workers at the Sunburst Children's Centre in Downsview, Ontario, summed up their complaint to the Task Force this way: "There is a Canada-wide subsidy in effect right now. We, the staff of centres throughout Canada, are the subsidy."

Only about 8% of day-care workers in licensed centres are protected by unions, and this shows.[19] The Katie Cooke Task Force found the mean wage of childcare workers in licensed centres to be $7.29 an hour in 1984. In Atlantic Canada the wage was lower—about $5 an hour. "Childcare workers," the Task Force said, "received only 64% of the salary of a mental retardation counsellor, and about 80% of that of a nursing assis-

---

18. Cooke, 1986, p. 112.

19. Moffatt, Patti Schom "The Bottom Line: Wages and Working Conditions of Workers in the Formal Day Care Market" Series 1, *Financing Child Care: Currnt Arrangements, a background paper for the Report of the Task Force on Child Care*, (Ottawa, Status of Women Canada 1986) pp. 85–150. The presence of a union was shown to have a major influence on wages; with the mean wage of unionized workers being 33% higher than that of non-unionized workers.

tant. In Ontario and Quebec, experienced childcare workers received only about half the wage of experienced elementary school teachers."[20] The task force neglected to say that in British Columbia general labourers, with no training or education whatever, were earning 35% more than the average daycare worker. Even employees looking after animals on government farms earned 35% more than childcare workers.[21]

In the past five years, especially in Quebec and Ontario, there have been substantial gains, notably with Ontario's direct operating grant to childcare centres. But for all that, the unmistakable societal message to childcare workers remains: you are both important and second-rate; we despise the good work that you do. Even as salaries rise, the low social status awarded to childcare workers remains an insult to them as well as the children in their care. "Why don't you institute minimum wage for this service?" Karen Bunker of Victoria asked the Task Force. "It's expected by someone who types letters all day, who works in a dry cleaners or wipes up toilets and floors for a living—are each of these more important than our children? If I made half what a garbageman makes, I could stay with the job—is our garbage more vital than our children? And who ever bothers to even consider it?"

Parental Ties

Another need of childcare is for parents to be on good terms with the daycare workers who see after their children.

Conflict between daycare and home can be almost as destructive as conflict between parents themselves in its isolation of children and neglect of their well-being. In that regard, one of the brilliant achievements of childcare advocates has been their ability to prevent disputes over staff salaries—persistently too low—from being a divisive factor between workers and parents. Peace was maintained partly by the fact that parents were clearly in charge and partly by a lack of jobs that forced workers to accept low salaries over unemployment. Workers also had close knowledge of parents' limits; they knew how hard it was to come up with $5,500 a year for a

---

20. Cooke, 1986, pp. 114, 115.
21. Moffatt, 1986, pp. 85–150.

child's care. So compromises were reached. But as workers get better and costlier educations, as the job market expands, and as salary demands move higher, friction is bound to result.

The way childcare workers ideally could work with parents was described by one worker who said she sees her centre as providing an extended family for the children. "I think it's up to the staff to make sure you include conversations with the child around the parent. If a child's fretty and crying, I say, 'It's really hard to say good-bye to your Mommy and Daddy when you love them so much and they love you, and it makes them sad to say good-bye too. Mommies and daddies don't really like going off to work and not seeing you all day long. That's not their favourite thing to do. But mommies and daddies work, and this is your place to be, and they'll be picking you up.' And then during the day I remind them about it, 'Gee, I'll bet your Mommy and Daddy are having lunch now, too.'

"You never try to take the place of, or belittle, a parent to the child. You never say, 'Well, that was a bad thing for your Mom or Dad to do.' Even if you feel that way—that maybe the drop-off time wasn't that supportive—you don't comment. You don't pass those judgmental kinds of thoughts along to the child.... I really see this daycare as an extended family unit."

This person works in a centre that pays each staff member a fair wage, allows them to work flexible shifts and four-day weeks, and had not had a staff member quit the centre in seven years.

Gender Equality

Men, as well as women, need to be involved in childcare. The lack of men's involvement is an almost universal family problem that has been dumped holus-bolus onto childcare. Very few of Canada's childcare workers are men; children remain for the most part as much in an underpaid and undervalued female ghetto as they were at home. Daycare is an extension of the domestic scene at home that remains deplorably debased in the public mind because of the deep currents of sexism that prevail. A remark of Fernand Daoust of the Quebec Federation of Labor to the House legislative committee in the fight against Bill C-144 explains the trouble. "Day care employees, for the most part women, earn very low wages and often have no job security, benefits or recognition," he declared. "As long as such work is seen as an extension of domestic work it will continue to be poorly appreciated." Which shows us how far we have to go on both accounts.

It is a problem that would decrease if childcare received the remuneration—the cold, hard cash, aside from all the accolades which people would rather give it—that it deserves. Men and women must equally participate in work and home, sharing what Freud called the great prescription for a happy life, "work and love." This concern needs to reach into labour policy as well as government regulation.

Miriam David and Caroline New suggest the quite sensible step of a shorter working day for all as a precondition for getting men involved in childcare. Instead of pressing for a four day week, as labour unions have been doing, shorter workdays may be a more humane option all around.[22] As David and New point out, work, childcare and parenthood all need to change. How do we start? They suggest turning upside down the current relationship of work to family, giving pride of place to family responsibilities in all our social relations. Childcare, they say, has to become a major public—rather than a purely private—concern; both women and men need to engage themselves both at home and in broader daycare concerns.

Another step is to recognize a taboo that keeps men at a distance from things domestic and is apparent in such simple things as dropping off children at a daycare centre. At one centre, mothers were observed coming in with their children, talking a while with the workers, signing the register, and starting their children at play, as if to establish a presence in the room. Then a father in a tan trench coat brought his child to the door and said "Okay, see you later, James," and was gone. James sauntered into the room past the clay table, the child-scale clus-

---

22. David, Miriam and Caroline New, "Feminist perspectives on childcare policy" in *Child Care and Equal Opportunities: some policy perspectives*, edited by Bronwen Cohen and Karen Clarke (London: Equal Opportunities Commission) p. 16.

ters of chairs, the doll and dress-up centre, to the library centre, took a book, plopped himself on the couch, and started looking at the pictures. Ten children and two attendants were in the room. None of them greeted James. He'd just been dropped off.

That abruptness wasn't true of all fathers. In fact, some workers pointed out that daycare breaks down the sharp separation of sex roles by offering some fathers more time to see their children—while delivering them to daycare. It takes a lot of undoing to break old conditioning. But the conditionings can fall aside as men realize their primary—and often neglected—human connection to that caring world, and start to rearrange their values and practices.

Cooperation, Not Competition

Children need to see an equal respect for themselves and others in the childcare setting. This seems a platitude, and that's often all it is. But to work it out in practice goes against much of the childcare that is given in our society—both inside and outside of families. The old hierarchical arrangement, in which one person is boss and the others do as told or in which adults sacrifice themselves for children who are then bound to them by enforced "gratitude," is not a democratic setting.

Changing that requires rethinking not just childcare but the power relationships that provide it. One example of a place that has tried to do this is the Friends Day Care Centre on Lowther Avenue in Toronto. Each of the four workers is paid at the same salary level, and each has an equal say in what goes on. None assumes the role of director; they work things out together. "I think the children don't see anyone as being the boss," Lynn Haines, one of the workers, said. "You may ask a child 'who's the boss around here' and the child will single out one of the staff, maybe because they see that person as most important to them. But they may say 'my Mom.' Or they may pick out another child." This practice frees each of the four staff members to do what she is good at in the group setting, and offers the children an example of a mutual sharing of gifts.

Another general rule at the centre is that children themselves make decisions about their affairs as far as they are able. The children had traditionally wrapped one of their own toys from home and brought it to a gift exchange at Christmas time. One mother had a better idea. She suggested to the staff that each child purchase a new toy instead and simply donate it to the centre. The staff told her, "That's an interesting idea. But of course we'll have to check it out with the children."

The children had a meeting about it, and they said no. They liked the old gift exchange, so that's how it stayed for the time being. This kind of thing makes democratic decision making more than a platitude without—and this is the other danger—allowing children to usurp the rightful, authoritative place of adults in the daycare situation. Self-government—at a level at which two-to-five-year-olds are capable—was a natural part of a system of fair play that the adults were trying to establish.

That is a far-cry from the rule of children. They had power over things they could handle, but adults remained clearly in charge. "We don't allow any violent play at all," Haines said. "No gun play of course, but no violent play. No jumping on each other or this attacking each other that kids do. It's a nonaggressive environment. Children are redirected in play.

"But they have choices. I would say something like, 'either we can find something else to do, and you need to change your play right now, or you can sit out for a while. That can be your choice, whichever you prefer to do.' They may decide to sit out (in the hall between the open doorways of the two main rooms)....

"Children of two-and-a-half or three will test that. They may decide they like sitting out, it sort of means they're growing up, they're rebelling, so they're going to sit out. They say, 'Well, I'm just going to sit here.' And then after while it's not so much fun so they choose to come back....

"We have a firm belief that children are social, that all humans are social, and want to be in a group... and that's where I see children willing to come back in. Their behaviour needs to be in respect to each other. And I think that comes across from the staff as well."

An old piece of folk wisdom: If children live with hostility, they learn to fight. If they live with criticism, they learn to condemn. If children live with fairness, they learn justice. If they live with approval, they learn to like themselves. And if they live with acceptance and friendship, they learn to find love in the world.

Part Of Society

Since daycare is a meeting place of private and public spheres, it is a place where elements of the wider society, too, are constantly at play. Daycare centres cannot, as families cannot, pretend outside influences do not penetrate to the centre of the institution.

Children need to be protected from the red-in-tooth-and-claw demands of the market economy, but they cannot be kept insulated from the impact of the outside world. But the outside world *can* be mediated and interpreted. One challenge of daycare is to help children to differentiate among the positive and negative forces at work in the world and to work out creative ways to exert their powers with others for the things they need and want.

At daycare it is not too early, for example, for group solidarity. In one centre we visited, there were no arbitrary groupings, either by age or by sex; the children were free to mingle as they chose; the only groups they formed were based on their own interests. But when a student worker decided one day to do a project with three-year-olds, excluding the two-year-olds, this caused a big disruption, with one two-year-old throwing a tantrum and the others wandering bewildered around the room. The children sensed something wasn't right. They were accustomed to an "inclusive" environment.

Nor is daycare too early for children to sense the power of feelings and find ways to put them to use with other people. Among nursery specialists the talk is about "developing language skills." This needs to be tied to the articulation of feelings, so that children understand their rightful power and effect.

At daycare, too, is a time to build the rewards and joys of personal friendships. At age four, children often fall powerfully under the spell of one another's presence; whether those first friendships are recognized and encouraged can make a large difference.

Those are some of the small things that can add up to a much larger struggle by the daycare community for equality, justice and a generosity of human interaction. Being part of the public sphere requires much more than teaching communication skills at the centre; it means declaring to the political and economic powers in society what we need from them to build a truly democratic, generous and loving community for children with adults. The struggle for good childcare will always have to take place on both private and public ground, but that is especially true now, at the starting stages, when public childcare has yet to be fully conceived.

Issues such as social class can be confronted all along the line, from the federal fight over equitable and generous granting formulae to the smallest matter of who pulls the toy cart to the playground. None of these things is negligible. Issues of social class pervade our environment, so they need to be acknowledged by adults both in the way we confront social reality and in the way we interact with children.

The same could be said of matters of race and gender and questions of patriotism, nationalism and imperialism. We should not impose these matters on small children as issues they must confront or work to solve, but neither do we shut our eyes to their impact on our children, nor to the creative ways children can learn to handle those issues as formulated in the real world of daycare.

One example of an issue being dealt with in a daycare occurred at the Friends Day Care Centre where the rules on violent play are strictly enforced. The children were at the playground, and Tommie and Steve were kicking a ball back and forth to each other. Tommie was almost three, Steve four. Things went fine for ten minutes. It was a free, loose romp around the playground. They threw it into a tree and watched it fall back through the branches.

Then they both ran for the ball at the same time, and Steve got it. Tommie stood on the curb of the wood-chip area and pointed his hand at Steve in the shape of a gun, thumb upward, and went "tsshew, tsshew, tsshew, tsshew."

At that moment a worker took Tommie by the hand. "You were angry at Steve for taking the ball and you were making gun games at him," she said. "You're going to have to figure out another way to let Steve know you're angry with him."

She took him to a park bench. "Now you are going to have to sit out and think about it."

Tommie, sober but unresisting, sat on the bench. About four minutes later he came walking back into the play area, where the worker again took his hand, and asked Steve, now on a swing, if Tommie could play with the ball. Steve said yes. The little episode was over.

It was a fragment of a larger lesson in the art of dealing with anger. Tommie was finding out that expressing anger in a symbolic, disengaged way through gun games doesn't work. It bottles up anger while giving it mock release, and leaves Tommie all the more isolated and powerless for not having learned to express anger in a way that gets results.

This was one example of how an astute worker, with good training and policy direction, can offer children the empowerment of their feelings—and a chance, in fact, to offer them as gifts.

An adult was in charge here, not in a distant, authoritarian way, but as a person among people who knew how to catch hold of their desires and direct them in ways that enabled them to be themselves with others.

The promotional material for this daycare centre says nothing about creating a positive self-image. But it says a lot about respecting children and teaching them how to care for and respect others. "To this end," it says, "we help them to learn non-violent friendly ways of communication and co-operation." That seemed to be exactly what it was about.

Childcare As A Gift

A key assumption of this book has been that the more loving, stable and just a community we can give our children, the better able they will be to build the strengths to be creative citizens.

We have tried not to paint this vision as a utopian dream. There is no point in make-believe. The painful truth is that most parents, as Michael Lerner has put it, "are refugees from the pain of their work experience and the pain of their childhoods." The "ideal" relationship between adults and children does not exist, but when we acknowledge the love and power that we have along with the tensions and hurts of contemporary life—at those moments we are probably closest to doing what we need to do. In fact, this vision is far less utopian, far more filled with human conflict and struggle, than the liberal "welfare/service" blueprint.

Yet it is also more democratic and stable. The other one hangs its trust on a technological system for delivering the social goods while ignoring our history as well as the need people have to give and receive in community and the creative power of that giving.

At the centre of this book we expressed the belief that children flourish best in a gift economy. The gift economy is one of exchange, but very different from the market economy. It does not seek personal profit. Instead, one offers gifts without attaching a value and without seeking a return, but knowing that a certain "debt of gratitude" is laid on the person who receives the gift. What that person does with the debt is wholly up to him or her. Gifts grow in value as they change hands—the sharing circle grows. So the gift that is given back or given on in the exchange circle becomes larger. That seems to be one of the keys to the evolution of human culture.

Gifts fully recognized and accepted are agents of change; they are "transformative." Those who receive gifts have a job on their hands, and the resulting return of gifts represents not just an expansion of the gifts but a potential transformation of those who have received. This is certainly true of those who open themselves to the gifts of children.

The very act of making the gift of a child to the world, at a primitive and basic level, is an act that shifts the balance. Having been given to, society has been obliged to give something back. Parents quite simply have laid on the rest of us a debt of gratitude. Something has been disrupted, thrown off balance. The world won't be the same place after this. We have here no mere commodity. This is a gift whose repercussions are unending.

That parents and children deserve public childcare is beyond question. That it be appropriate to their needs is important and must be worked out. But that it could form a part of a major gift exchange in Canadian society, in which the innate and unquestioned gifts of children are met with a generous "return gift" by those who love and care for them—that would be a startling and life-giving transformation.

Join The Debate On What Should Happen In Canada's Schools. You Can Still Get Your Own Copy Of Each Of These Issues Of Our Schools/Our Selves.

Issue #1: (Journal) A Feminist Agenda For Canadian Education ... The Saskatoon Native Survival School ... School Wars: BC, Alberta, Manitoba ... Contracting Out At The Toronto Board ... On Strike: Toronto Teachers And Saskatoon Profs ... Labour's Message in Nova Scotia Schools and Queen's Park ... The Free Trade Ratchet ...

Issue #2: Educating Citizens: A Democratic Socialist Agenda For Canadian Education by Ken Osborne. A coherent curriculum policy focussed on "active citizenship." Osborne takes on the issues of a "working-class curriculum" and a national "core" curriculum: what should student's know about Canada and the world at large?

Issue #3: (Journal) BC Teachers, Solidarity and Vander Zalm ... The Anti-Streaming Battle in Ontario ... The Dangers of School-Based Budgeting ... "Whole Language" in Nova Scotia ... Vancouver's Elementary Schools 1920-60 ... The Martimes in Song and Text ... Teaching "G-Level" Kids ... The Squeeze on Alberta's Teachers ... In Winnipeg: "The Green Slime Strikes Back!" ...

Issue #4: (Journal) Teaching The Real Stuff Of The World: Bears, History, Work Skills ... Tory Times At Sask Ed ... The NDP At The Toronto School Board ... Indian Control In Alberta Schools ... Is The Action Affirmative For Women School Board Workers ... Radwanski: The Dark Side ... More On "Whole Language" In Nova Scotia ... A Steelworker's Education ... B.C. Teachers Hang Tough ... Decoding Discrimination ...

Issue #5: Making A People's Curriculum: The Experience Of La maîtresse d'école edited with an introduction by David Clandfield. Since 1975 this Montreal teacher collective has been producing alternative francophone curricula on labour, human rights, peace, and geo-political issues in a framework of cooperative learning. This is an anthology of their best work.

Issue #6: (Journal) Labour Education And The Auto Workers ... Nova Scotia's Children Of The State ... Patrick Watson's *Democracy* ... Popular Roots Of The "New Literacy" ... Canada's Learner Centres ... Right Wing Thinking In Education ... Fighting Sexism In Nfld ... The Computer Bandwagon ... *Glasnost* and *Perestroika* Over Here? Funding Native Education ...

Issue #7: Claiming An Education: Feminism and Canadian Schools by Jane Gaskell, Arlene McLaren, Myra Novogrodsky. This book examines "equal opportunity," what students learn about women, what women learn about themselves and what has been accomplished by women who teach, as mothers and teachers.

Issue #8: It's Our Own Knowledge: Labour, Public Education & Skills Training by Julie Davis et al. The clearest expression yet of Labour's new educational agenda for the 1990s. It begins with working class experience in the schools and community colleges, takes issue with corporate initiatives in skills training, and proposes a program "for workers, not for bosses."

Issue #9: (Journal) Rekindling Literacy In Mozambique ... Privatizing The Community Colleges ... CUPE's Educational Agenda ... High Schools & Teenage Sex ... Workers And The Rise of Mass Schooling ... More On Nova Scotia's Children of the State ... Grade 1 Learning ... Private School Funding ... The Globe's Attack on Media Studies ... "Consolidation" in PEI ... Manitoba's High School Review ...

Issue #10: Heritage Languages: The Development And Denial Of Canada's Linguistic Resources by Jim Cummins and Marcel Danesi. This book opens up the issue of teaching heritage languages in our schools to a broad audience. It provides the historical context, analyzes opposing positions, examines the rationale and research support for heritage language promotion, and looks at the future of multiculturalism and multilingualism in Canada.

Issue #11: (Journal) No More War Toys: The Quebec Campaign ... Labelling the Under-Fives ... Building a Socialist Curriculum ... High School Streaming in Ontario ... Growing Up Male in Nova Scotia ... New Left Academics ... Tory Cutbacks in Alberta ... More On Workers And The Rise Of Mass Schooling ... The Elementary School Ruby And How High School Turned Her Sour ...

Double Issue #12-13: What Our High Schools Could Be: A Teacher's Reflections From The 60s To The 90s by Bob Davis. The author leads us where his experience has led him — as a teacher in a treatment centre for disturbed children, in an alternative community school, in a graduate education faculty, and for 23 years in two Metro Toronto high schools. The book ranges from powerful description to sharp analysis — from sex education to student streaming to the new skills mania.

Issue #14: (Journal) Feminism, Schools and the Union ... What's Happening in China's Schools ... NB Teacher Aides and the Struggle for Standards ... Barbie Dolls and Unicef ... Post-secondary Cuts in Alberta ... CUPE-Teacher Links ... Language Control In Nova Scotia ... Pay Equity For Ontario Teachers ... Women's Struggles/Men's Responsibility ...

Issue #15: Cooperative Learning And Social Change: Selected Writings Of Célestin Freinet edited and translated by David Clandfield and John Sivell. Célestin Freinet (1896-1966) pioneered an international movement for radical educational reform through cooperative learning. His pedagogy is as fresh and relevant today as it was in his own time, whether dealing with the importance of creative and useful work for children or linking schooling and community with wider issues of social justice and political action. This translation is the first to bring a broad selection of Freinet's work to an English-speaking audience.

Issue #16: (Journal) BC's Privatization Of Apprenticeship ... Marketing Adult Ed In Saskatchewan ... The Future Of Ontario's CAATs ... Edmonton's Catalyst Theatre ... The Money Crisis In Nova Scotia Schools ... The Politics Of Children's Literature ... Tough Kids Out Of Control ... A Literacy Policy For Newfoundland? ... Métis Schooldays ... Capitalism And Donald Duck ... In Struggle: Ontario Elementary Teachers ...

Issue #17: (Journal) Towards An Anti-Racist Curriculum ... Discovering Columbus ... The Baffin Writers' Project ... The Anti-Apartheid Struggle In South Africa's Schools ... What People Think About Schooling ... Children's Work ... Radical Literacy ... Getting the Gulf Into The Classroom ... Bye-Bye Minimum C Grades ... Taking Action On Aids ...

Issue #18: (Journal) Can The NDP Make A Difference? ... Columbus In Children's Literature ... Labour Takes On Ontario's Education Bureaucrats ... Lessons From Yukon Schools ... Vision 2000 Revisited ... Getting A Feminist Education The Hard Way ... Children In Poverty ... Reflections Of A Lesbian Teacher ... Literacy, Politics and Religion in Newfoundland ... Critiquing the National Indicators ... Student Loans In Saskatchewan ...

Double Issue #19-20: Teaching For Democratic Citizenship by Ken Osborne. In this book Osborne extends his work in *Educating Citizens* and takes us through the world of modern pedagogies and the most recent research on effective teaching. He focuses particularly on "discovery learning," "critical pedagogy," and "feminist pedagogy" — drawing from a wide range of classroom practice — and builds on this foundation the key elements of an approach to teaching in which democratic citizenship is the core of student experience.

Issue #21: (Journal) The Tory Agenda ... Higher Education For Sale ... Racism and Education: Fighting Back in Nova Scotia, in a Scarborough Collegiate, in South Africa and in Victoria's Chinese Student Strike ... Saskatchewan's Neo-Conservatives ... As Neutral As My Teacher, Jesus ... "Make Work" in New Brunswick ... Teachers Politics: In Ontario and Mexico ... A Feminist Presence ... Canada's Heritage Language Programs.